Dear

**Wartime letters sent from a
Scottish mother to her son**

John B White

MAPLE
PUBLISHERS

Dear John

Author: John B White

Copyright © 2024 John B White

The right of John B White to be identified as author of this work has been asserted by the author in accordance with section 77 and 78 of the Copyright, Designs and Patents Act 1988.

First Published in 2024

ISBN 978-1-83538-268-4 (Paperback)
      978-1-83538-269-1 (Hardback)
      978-1-83538-270-7 (E-Book)

Book cover design and Book layout by:
      White Magic Studios
      www.whitemagicstudios.co.uk

Published by:
      Maple Publishers
      Fairbourne Drive, Atterbury,
      Milton Keynes,
      MK10 9RG, UK
      www.maplepublishers.com

A CIP catalogue record for this title is available from the British Library.

This book is a memoir. It reflects the author's recollections of experiences over time. Some names and characteristics have been changed, some events have been compressed, and some dialogues have been recreated, and the Publisher hereby disclaims any responsibility for them.

Introduction

As I start this book, I am trying to think of the last occasion I took the time to take a pen and paper to write a proper letter, then place it in an envelope, address it, buy and stick on the stamp and post it. Many years ago I think.

Nowadays it's all texting, WhatsApping, emailing and social media posting. In this digital age the art of writing a letter is a rapidly diminishing one.

Perhaps because we write our short comments, quick messages and so forth on computer platforms we value it less. Messages are riddled with typing errors as it seems our busy lives prevents us from taking a few minutes checking over what we have written. We probably spend little time thinking about what we are writing, it's all got to be done quickly. We hit 'send' and off it goes into the internet ether, and we think nothing of it. It's gone, job done. The advent of digital platforms has enabled us to communicate quicker and more easily but the personal and emotional touch of a physical letter has all but disappeared.

Possibly this technological development making communication faster and simpler has led people to think that writing a letter is a waste of their valuable time. We seldom ever print out the email on actual paper. At the other end the recipient reads the words quickly and no doubt to save computer space deletes it thus destroying our written words. We often don't even respond to messages we read on somewhere like Facebook apart from hitting the like button.

Of course, this is a personal view but think of the thrill you once got when the postman popped a letter through the letter box, not a bill, and you recognised the writing as from someone in the family or a friend, perhaps it was a love letter from a boyfriend or girlfriend. The eager anticipation of opening the envelope and sitting down to read the contents. Of course, the letter may contain bad news but still someone had taken the time to sit and write to you.

So, the art and habit of writing letters is a rapidly diminishing one. It appears that the days of families and friends keeping in touch and updating each other on how life was treating them through written correspondence has almost gone.

The idea for this book came about when going through old documents my sister and I had in our possession, much was correspondence written when letter writing was much more common than today. It appears that my mother and father kept many letters that they had received during their lifetime: the letters I had written to my parents from America in the seventies containing details of events that I had completely forgotten about, letters from my Uncle Kenneth to my mother's mother as he lay in a Nursing Home trying to be cured of Tuberculosis in the 1930s letters of sympathy to my grandparents when he died in 1939, love letters from my father to my mother just after I had been born and the war time correspondence my grandmother sent to my father serving in the RAF during World War 2.

One of my regrets in life occurred in the 1980s not long after getting married and having children. I had in my possession many letters sent from girlfriends and friends in America after my time there. On a fateful Sunday afternoon, I decided that the past was gone, and it was time to look to the future, so I destroyed those communications in which was so much information about people dear to me and of my life as a young man. Thankfully my mother and father did not do this.

This short volume concentrates only on my grandmother's war letters to my father. Letters from a loving mother to her son keeping him abreast of everything that was happening back home. I can imagine my father receiving these wherever he was stationed and the smile on his face as he began reading the contents.

Like many aspects of letter writing these letters include how the family is getting on, the weather and of course who is ill or passed away.

But as they were set in the war many references are made of events, some locally and others nationally. I have copied them as they were written including the many Scottish terms used and the omission of punctuation. A glossary of Scottish words used, and their meanings can be found at the end of the book.

They were mainly posted from the Scottish town of Ayr, situated on the coast about 40 miles south of Glasgow and standing on the Firth of Clyde. At one time it was a very popular destination for holidaymakers due to its long sandy beach and assorted attractions and before the advent of cheap air travel. Many aspects of life in Ayr are mentioned in the letters, a town at the time with a population between 30,000 and 40,000.

The town's population was always swollen in July due to the Glasgow Fair which saw many people from the city come to Ayr for their holidays. The billeting of soldiers and evacuated children from Glasgow would also have increased the numbers.

It was a busy fishing port and harbour at the time of war and had several factories. It was also a market town with a large farmer's market taking place on Tuesdays.

The Low Green near Ayr Beach. The building on the left is Ayr Pavilion.

I have endeavoured to include dates when the correspondence was written although not every letter included the year. For those without a date I have used the information within the letter to place it within a war year. Only one, the first letter, can not be definitively given a year but I have gone for 1941.

The letters were mainly written from the family home, a bungalow, at 1 Lothian Rd. The main correspondent is my grandmother Nellie and although I never met her as she died before I was born, I have learned a lot about the woman through her words and I trust the reader will develop their own thoughts as to the type of woman she was as well as other family members. During this time John's father and several of his siblings chipped in with a few lines here and there.

I have also added photographs of my father's family and images he took while on service, mainly in Egypt and which he kept in a scrapbook. There are also a few I have taken on a few visits to Ayr in recent years.

An airmail letter cover and the address where they were sent.

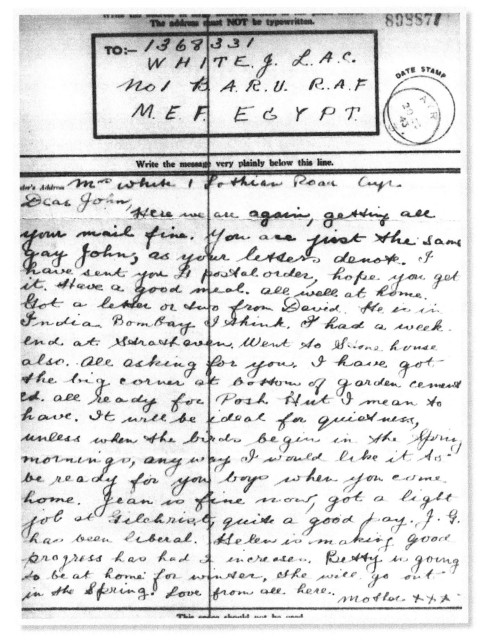

The address must NOT be typewritten. 899887

TO:- 1368331
WHITE. J. L.A.C.
No1 B.A.R.U. R.A.F
M.E.F. EGYPT.

DATE STAMP

Write the message very plainly below this line.

Sender's Address Mrs White 1 Lothian Road Cup.

Dear John,
Here we are again, getting all
your mail fine. You are just the same
gay John, as your letters denote. I
have sent you a postal order, hope you get
it. Have a good meal. All well at home.
Got a letter or two from David. He is in
India. Bombay I think. I had a weekend at Strathaven. Went to Stone house
also. All asking for you. I have got
the big corner at bottom of garden cement-
ed. All ready for Posh Hut I mean to
have. It will be ideal for quietness,
unless when the birds begin in the Spring
mornings, anyway I would like it to
be ready for you boys when you come
home. Jean is fine now, got a light
job at Gilchrist, quite a good pay. J.G.
has been liberal. Helen is making good
progress has had a increase. Betty is going
to be at home for winter, she will go out
in the Spring. Love from all here. Mother xxx

One of my grandmother's airgraphs sent to my father.

The Family

As stated in the introduction most of the letters written were from my grandmother Helen White (nee Gibson) although she was always known as Nellie. Here and there members of the family chip in a few lines.

Helen was born in 1890 in Ayr, but lived for most of her childhood years in the small Ayrshire town of Beith where her father was a cabinet maker.

She married David White in 1911 and had their first child, Willie, in 1912.

She was in her fifties when these letters were written, and many mentions are made on how she made her money through letting rooms in her home. It would appear in one letter that 4 rooms were let out which I find difficult to understand as the house was not huge and as well as Nellie and her husband, 3 of the daughters were at home. Where everyone slept is anyone's guess although I do know a garden hut was utilised by pop.

In the letters David is known as 'pop' as well as a few less complimentary names. He was born in 1889 in the Lanarkshire town of Hamilton where his father, William Dickson White was a baker. David followed in his father's footsteps in this profession. During the war he was working for Gilchrist the Bakers in Ayr where he was a foreman. He received many awards for his bread making skills.

The family consisted of David, Nellie and 7 children, Jean, Nan, Willie, David, John my father, Helen and Betty the youngest.

Initially the family had resided at 25 George's Avenue in Ayr before moving to Lothian Rd. which lies near Ayr's town centre.

1 Lothian Rd. as it is today.

My father had been born in Ayr in 1920 and was the middle child of 7. On leaving school he began working for Boots the Chemist and when war broke out was in training to become a pharmacist. He joined the RAF, possibly in 1941, and became an aircraft fitter serving in South Africa, Egypt and Greece.

Willie had been born in 1912 and was the eldest. He was married to Jean Conkie in 1936. He was at home throughout the war, but his occupations changed throughout those years as can be read about in the letters. At this time the letters begin he and Jean had two children, David and Alice. Another child came along in 1944.

Nan was my father's older sister although her real name was Agnes. She was born in 1914. She had married Bill Cowan in 1934 and like Willie by the time war started had two children, Ronald and Roxie. Her husband was serving in the far east.

Jean was another sister, born in 1921 and living at home at the time. From clues within the letters, she signed up when the war started and for a while was serving the army in some capacity but was discharged due to health reasons and throughout the war had several jobs.

David, like my father, was serving with the RAF although in what capacity the letters do not make clear although it is likely that he too was an aircraft fitter. He was unmarried but as can be seen in the correspondence had an English girlfriend called Joyce who came from a Suffolk town called Clare.

My father's two younger sisters were Helen and Betty. Helen was living at home and working, although she was in her early teens. Betty, the youngest of the family, was born in 1928 and still a schoolchild when the letters begin, attending Ayr Grammar school where she consistently seems to have been at the top of the class.

The letters begin in 1941 after my father had signed up with the RAF. Why he chose this arm of the services or became an aircraft fitter I do not know. Questions that should have been asked of him as well as his war exploits many years ago.

At this point I do not know if my father had been posted overseas or was still training in the United Kingdom. I suspect he was not abroad as it appears my grandmother was sending him items of clothing which was probably not possible when he was serving abroad. Another clue is that the letter was written on normal paper and not in airmail format.

Back Row – John, Nan, Willie, Jean and David

Front row – Helen, David Sr, Nellie and Betty

My grandmother, Nellie

My father in RAF uniform

The Letters
1941

Many of the first letters do not have dates on them but being written on normal paper seem to indicate they were written near the beginning of the war and probably 1941. They obviously may not be in chronological order.

Dear John,

Your letter received okay. Glad you arrived safe. Have you been home?? Sometimes I think I have been dreaming, it went in so quickly, and I hardly got talking to you. Anyway one thing I know you are looking very well. So that pleased me. A pity the shinty was on Sunday, I was only worried about the wee boy crying as I thought these gomerils* out at the back had hurt him. Jean's bad temper will have had time to cool. I am quite sure by now she will be sorry at what she did but I bear her no ill will, but she can make the first move. She thinks I did the planning about Sunday's work at the bakery, well as you know it was pop. She will take the extra money in her pay, that will be an insight for you so watch out for the right girl when she comes along. They most of them are twisters. Well John will you see about your allowance money, make inquiries the girl in the P.O. said. Ask your community officer about it. James Gilchrist had been talking to your father and he is going to give him a bonus in a fortnight's time, when the books come back from the auditors. But believe me he will have made a good bit so here's hoping and I will put some in the bank for you to jaunt about on your next leave. I have told them that the children are to be kept to their own rooms when the boys are here as we like a little peace and time to sit and talk. Well you can forget Sunday, what a pant.

Our Jean will need to register as she is 20. Perhaps she should volunteer and get into something suitable. Do you know who was killed. David Pringle the auctioneer. A motor smash. His wife is in Kilmarnock Infirmary seriously ill. Well John I will send on your wee breeks* on Monday and maybe some fruit cakes. I'll need to buy them as I cannot get currants. Jimmy Orr says his son is missing. He was flying over London for a six hours trial, they have heard no word of him but he might still be alright. Cheerio John and watch your step. I'll be writing you a note on Monday. Did David send you his address. Here it is in case he did not.

D White 951065

214 Squadron

Stradis Hall

Clare

Suffolk

That will be a nice place likely. Lovely countryside. When we have a car we will visit there.

Love from mother x x

It appears that some sort of bust up occurred between mother and daughter. What Jean did must remain a mystery. Who the 'gomerils' were and why the little boy was upset must also remain unknown.

David's address is significant in that the town of Clare in Suffolk is where he met his future wife.

Dear John,

Enclosed are some chocolates that Willie has made for you. We hope you will enjoy them. Willie is on holiday but the weather is so cold, we are just hanging around the fire. Got your letter on Saturday alright. I was away a run on Monday to Kilmarnock with Agnes to see Mrs McKerrow. Nice wee house she has, very comfortable. Well John Willie is waiting to get away with the parcel to the Post Office so excuse this short letter.. Enclosed money will get you a nice tea somewhere. Hope you are well and still behaving yourself. We had the jerries over north east Scotland, getting kind of near again.

Love from all at Lothian Rd.

John's brothers, Willie and David

Tuesday

Dear John,

Your letter received with money order safely. As you say it will come in handy for your holidays. What a night we had last night, raiders passing over. Clydeside got it again and there are cancellations at

Kilmarnock, so I'll bet we get a dose of it before long. We were wakened on Sunday morning with the alert, the all clear did not sound until 3.30 Sunday morning. What a nerve racking time. I wish it was all over and living in peace again. The weather here is good, it is fine to sit around in the sun. I have got an old couple for a week, they are from Paisley. Well John there is little in the way of news. We are carrying on as usual so here's hoping we see you soon. Trust you will have good weather when you come. Willie has been using your bike. I better give him the will to have it cleaned up for you coming back. So cheerio meantime. Love from all at home. Faither was dressed up on Monday afternoon to give us a laugh. Whit a sight. Mrs Kerr was in fits laughing at him.

Love from mother.

This letter was undated but as mention of the Clydebank Blitz I have put it as March 1941 as that is when this event occurred. The town of Kilmarnock lies around 15 miles from Ayr and is passed by on route to Scotland's largest city.

The Clydebank Blitz took place on the nights of 13 and 14 March 1941 with the targets being the John Brown Shipyard, ROF Dalmuir, a government owned Ordnance factory and the Singer Corporation Factory particular targets. The Singer factory had ceased making sewing machines due to the war and had begun to make weapons. Clydebank, a town near Glasgow, was largely destroyed and it suffered the worst destruction and civilian loss of life in all of Scotland. The death toll was 1,200 people with 1,000 seriously injured. Hundreds more were injured by blast debris. Over the course of the two nights, a total of 439 Luftwaffe bombers dropped in excess of 1,650 incendiary containers and 272 tonnes of bombs. Out of approximately 12,000 houses, only eight remained undamaged, with 4,000 destroyed and 4,500 severely damaged. Over 35,000 people were made homeless.

I am uncertain as to the meaning of my grandmother's mention of my father's girlfriend and why 'pop' would be 'selling farms'.

31st March

Normal letter

Dear John,

Just a few lines with your pants. They are not much worth. I will need to get you another pair soon. Well we are all jogging along as usual at Ayr. I was away a run on, Monday with Barr Rankine Tours, over the hill and far away. I enjoyed it fine, it was a change. I travelled alone, that suits me fine. Nae body to argue with. I mean to be doing a lot of touring this summer all going well.

Betty as you will see has had the mumps, so she got a fortnight off the school and they get their holidays this week so that will be another 10 days for her.

We might be going to Strathaven for a few days for a change of air. It would do Betty good. We have had 2 visits of Dr Brand and have to watch for cold winds. Heat is the thing for mumps.

What about keeping a record of all your sweeties. It would make good reading in future years.

So far have not got your allowance notice yet. Have you made enquiries about it yet. Well it will be worth getting it in a lump and it is to go to the bank, you will certainly need cash when your leave comes round, not much fun when the pockets are empty. I am writing to David also. I like to get your letters away at the beginning of the week not that there is much news.

Mrs Goode is away home now, it was a rest for her but as she says one must carry on at home. There has been no raids since the Clydebank Blitz but we had better not hope too much.

Well John I'll need to get faither's dinner ready. He was fire watching on Saturday night. I think the fun would be good. Hope you are getting on alright and don't be blawing* to your girlfriend about the farms you father has to sell up in Scotland.

Johnnie Wilson left £1441. That would be the insurance in that and the bungalow he bought outright for cash when they flitted from Boswell Park.

Love from mother

Why my father's 'sweeties' would make interesting reading is unknown. Perhaps it is a reference to girls my father was seeing although he never told me about any 'sweethearts' when he was a young man.

My grandmother allowed visitors to stay in the home on their holidays charging I believe about £3 a week. (Today that would be £126.) Through the letters I believe she prided herself on being a good landlady. I would suspect that Mrs Goode had been one such customer.

Unknown date

Normal letter

Dear John,

Just a few lines as I did not write last week. Yes I got £3 odd from Boots, but I have not received your allowance book. Will I get notified through the post that it is ready at the post office? I think that is what I got for Davy's. If I remember right you said you would like it in the post office. It would be great if David managed with you.

We are all jogging along as usual. I was looking in Boots the other day, they seemed to be very busy. Did you get your teeth fixed alright? I am looking forward to your leave. I am going out a walk to Mrs ???? this afternoon it being Sunday. Leezie *(Betty)* has made the dinner, I feel an awful smell of burning, the turnip had boiled dry. I tell her she will need to be a good cook and look after me in my old age. Helen can get the swell job. They will write you end of the week as exams are on.

That was Kenneth in just now and he was saying that David's parcel had been returned to them so that is not so bad. They are going to send him on the gloves and fags. The rest of the stuff was wasted, cakes.

Yon chap Thomson who sang in the choir is missing. His father was a woodwork teacher. He was a pilot in the air force.

Well John I have no more news. Enclosed is 10/- that will help you along so don't spend it daft. Something to eat as I can't be bothered baking yet. Love from all.

Mother

Willie was fire watching on Saturday night. Pop says he will get a fireman's suit when he is on duty. Always the fool.

Kenneth mentioned in the letter was my father's cousin. He was the son of one of Nellie's sisters.

My father had worked in Boot's before the war and there seemed to be some arrangement where he still got paid even though he was now in the RAF.

Regarding the fire watching, Ayr was never really bombed as mentioned earlier. Air raid siren drills took place regularly and a black out naturally was in force. It is strange that the German air force seemed to ignore the town as it had a very busy harbour, some engineering works and a large naval training unit just south of the town. The RAF had a base at Prestwick and the American air force also ferried in Liberator Bombers as well as supply planes to the airfield at Prestwick. In total 37,000 military aircraft arrived at Prestwick during the war years.

On the one occasion in September in either 1942 or 1943 a German plane dropped a landmine just outside Ayr Harbour which produced a huge bang and scared those who heard it. Fortunately, no one was killed not any damage done. I was told that when this happened, and the town sirens sounded, my grandfather ran all the way home and hid under the bed until the 'all clear' was sounded.

The river Ayr flowing into the Forth of Clyde. In war time the harbour would have been filled with boats. The landmine would have been dropped near where the river disappears from view in the photograph.

Unknown date

Normal letter

Dear John,

Your letter received today, Saturday. Glad you are enjoying the sweets. We are all in our usual at Ayr. It is very busy here, a lot of extra people wherever they have come from. Father is very busy making bread just as busy as the Glasgow Fair.

I have got a couple in the front bedroom now. She was a nurse before the war, married and has travelled to many places with the toffs. She has been at Monte Carlo, Vienna etc and Tunbridge Wells. She was 9 years in London in the West End. She is 49 years of age and what a nice person. Her husband is a joiner in the shipyard, and he is being transferred from Glasgow to Ayr. So I have been very lucky and she is so pleased to have got into such a nice room. I have nothing to do for her and I get 22/6 for the room per week, 1/- extra for gas and she buys her own coal so that is £4/10/- per month and I am rent free which suits me.

I had to stop just now to answer the door, a lady and her daughter for the weekend in the parlour so I put the fire on and made up the bed, and I get my guinea for that on Monday night so that is the benefit of a nice place to live, you can always turn a pound. So Jock upwards and onwards. Let that be your password.

I was being introduced to Mr Kerr, the lady's husband. He has just arrived and he is a nice man. Pop will have someone to chat with now. Father is very tired at the weekend. Pity he had not saved his money better and been able to retire sometime. Ach well he is happy at work.

Well you know Jean that fair haired girl that stays with Aunt Caddell. She has got engaged to a widower, a brother of yon Jimmy Creedie that works with father. Another brother, Ron McReedie got the jail for bigamy. You have heard father talk of him. Fancy getting in among a lot like that. He has 4 of a family. One of the girls works besides Jean in the boot shop. That is where Jean met him. He came into the shop to talk to his girl and was introduced to Jean. Nice looking girl like her could have got a nice chap. He is a sergeant in the army. So we will see how that romance turns out. She got the ring this week as he was on leave.

Helen is starting in Burtons next week and then typing in the evenings. Well John I will dry up. I have got no money from the government yet for you but it will be fine if you get it for your next leave. We will make it go on jaunts. I dare say you will feel the work a bit baffling, do your best, you can do no more. You will all be glad to get home after this blasted war is over. I wonder when that will be. I am feeling a lot better, making a pound is a good tonic for me. Hope you are still in the pink.

Love from all at home. Mother x

The fact that my grandmother thinks John will be finding the work baffling makes me think that this was written not long after he started his training.

Unknown date
Normal letter

Dear John,

Just a note to say I got your letter. What a treat to meet the *(the next word looks like Damwit but unlikely to be so whoever it was is unclear.)* I had a letter from him and he says you are looking so swell.

I am getting on fine, the rest has done me good. I have written to the girls telling them I won't be able to take them back. I don't think they will get back to Mary Loudon's anyway. Too long to keep their job open. Nance Caddell was in this morning with a lovely bit of fish done to perfection. Did I enjoy it? Yes sir. So I'll not be so keen on flying around for a time working but rest and quietness for a woman of 50. There is such a strain on the system that life has to be taken quietly. Old pop would not have the brains to understand that, a lot of dam blethers, he would say. Well I take things easy now. Leave it to a Gibson to be fly.

There was a big fire out at the aerodrome at Prestwick, quite a lot hurt. I hear from David you look great and the guid* laugh you had. Well John the weather here is awful. I'm longing for the nice one and yours truly will be the lady for a change, no letting with attendance this year. Doon* the shore and a deck chair will do me. Will be looking forward to seeing you some day soon.

Alice, Jean's sister, comes over daily and does the work and I rest and eat.

Love from mother

Alice was Willie's sister-in-law.

I think the girls must have been lodgers at Lothian Rd. and perhaps worked in the town although it must remain unidentified what 'Mary Loudon's' was.

Dad and his mate Bert Catto, also from Ayr, in the tented camp, Heliopolis.

1942

Air Graphs

At this point my grandmother began writing using airgraphs.

In the early months of World War 2 the ministry of transport in GB was faced with serious problems in maintaining a postal service for forces stationed in the middle east where my father was.

Mail could only be sent there by air, but space was extremely limited and letters by sea were taking 3 to 6 months to reach their destination. The post office realized that the solution could be lie in the Kodak microfilm system. Thus, the airgraph was born. The basic concept was simple. The letters were photographed at the sending end and the negatives sent to their destination by air. Then the negatives were turned into 'airgraphs' by the company Kodak and sent on to the recipient. The Kodak office in Cairo already had the necessary equipment to do the task. The service started on April 21st, 1941.

6th April 1942

Airgraph

My dear John,

Have received all your airgraphs so this is my first attempt. Hope it turns out o.k. This is Easter week. We are all well here. David comes on leave 21st April. Yes we got your photo from Durban. Nan has got word that Bill is posted as missing but we are all living in the hope that he is a prisoner. Pop is now making the National Bread.

This is Easter week. H & B are on holiday. We have got all our spring cleaning done so I am now ready to get off my mark on the sunny days. I cast longing looks at Boots when I pass but there is someone not there. Mr Gillieson the minister has died. Jim Johnson is now overseas. I am glad you are well John. You will get a good holiday when you come home. Let's hope it won't be so very long till I see you at the door. We will watch for you in the Newsreels.

Betty is first in the class this term so the reward is a new costume. Well John you are always in my thoughts and I just live for the day you will be safe at home. Watch your health when the hot weather comes. Love from all at home. Willie is writing you. Hope you saw Alan Paterson. Cheerio, all my love to you.

Mother x

This communication also had no year stamped on it but due to the mention of pop starting to make National bread it must be 1942 when the bread began to be produced.

The National Loaf was a bread made from wholemeal flour with added calcium and vitamins, introduced in Britain during the War by the Federation of Bakers in 1942. The loaf (similar to today's brown bread) was made from wholemeal flour to combat wartime shortages of white flour and sugar.

Working with the government, the FOB published four recipes for wholemeal bread, which became the only recipes that could legally be used to make bread in the U.K. The National Loaf was grey, mushy and unappetising; only one person in seven preferred it to white bread, which became unavailable. The government insisted on it as it saved space in ships carrying food to Britain and allowed better utilization of existing stocks of wheat. The loaf was abolished in October 1956.

South Africa may have been a rather out of the way place then for my father to be posted but the country was used by the RAF for training purposes, so I presume he went there to learn his trade.

It is also the first mention of Nan's husband Bill going missing in the Far East. He had been captured by the Japanese, but the family did not know this for several months. The person missing from Boots would be my father as this was where he worked before the war.

H & B were Nelie's daughters Helen and Betty.

My father, left, with his friend Jacky enjoying some leisure time in Durban.

16th April 1942

Airgraph

Dear John,

Here we are again giving you our latest news. Had a letter from Ivy. She would like to come again this year so it will be ok. I am getting the old ledger out for return bookings of my visitors. I have had 4 requests already.

The garden is a picture John, all set for David's leave. He is now L.A.C. White, so the local boys make good.

Had a letter from Bill, it had been written after Xmas.. Nan has had no word yet, rather an anxious time. Sorry you had been in hospital. I bet you were wishing you were at home. It's a weary wait, I'll put up with it if I get you safely back.

Mrs McMurdo sends you her best wishes. Pop is getting another scream of a letter ready for you., dealing mostly with the spring cleaning problems he had to face. Well it was worth it. 1 Lothian Rd. is looking its best both outside and in. Helen and Betty are growing fast, quite the young ladies now with new costumes. Well John, all for the present.

All my love to you, mother x

It is not known what John was in hospital for although it does not sound as if it was serious.

The letters L.A.C. for Willie in the RAF stands for Leading Aircraftman. It was actually the third lowest rank with only Aircraftsman 1ˢᵗ and 2ⁿᵈ Class below this, but Nellie was still a proud mum.

10ᵗʰ May 1942

Airgraph

Dear John,

Received your last airgraph o.k. I am getting all booked up for the summer business, mostly return bookings, 4ᵗʰ year for some of them. When the war is over I'll try and get Bellisle House or Craigie. I had a letter from Bill a while back. He said it would be a swell idea to start a boarding house, so here's hoping. I think a Hydro would be better John, you could mix the pills for the various complaints. Plooks* on the broo* etc.

I wish you could see the lilac tree in the garden. I'll try and get a snap of it for you. Hope you are well. David is away back after the leave. We were at the Gaiety with him. It was Harry Gordon. What a laugh. Well here's to the next time. All my love to you John and look after yourself.

Mother x

It is not certain this is from 1942 as no year is stamped on the airgraph. Bill was my father's sister Nan's husband. He was reported missing in an airgraph sent on 6th April so it could be she is referring to an earlier time. It can't be 1941 as her first airgraph was on 6th April 1942.

The Gaiety was Ayr's main theatre and had opened in 1902. After World War 1 it was a cinema before being bought by Ben Popplewell who was from Bradford and already owned Ayr Pavilion. In 1935 the theatre was remodelled and was most well known for it's summer shows entitled the 'The Gaiety Whirl' with many well know Scottish starts appearing there. It also staged pantomimes and serious plays. Mr Popplewell and his family ran the theatre for over 50 years.

One family link appears to be that pop White on several occasions got up on the stage and entertained the audience with amusing stories and songs although how this came about is not known. Perhaps they had open nights where people in the audience could perform an act.

Ayr Pavilion

22nd June 1942

Airgraph

Dear John,

Here we are at Edinburgh on holiday. Lovely place and very busy. I am enjoying myself fine with Helen and Betty. I am going today to see if I can send the money from here. I see they have a Cook's place in Princes St. We will go home on Saturday and David will be arriving with his girl. Did I tell you she writes poetry? Let's hope she is not too high brow. Saw a nice picture last night. Greer Garson in 'Random Harvest'.

I have a busy month in July. Nan is over keeping house for me. Roxie had been looking at a snap of her grandpa and said 'Bad old man. Granny told me'. Loud laughs from all. Is she not the wee sweet lassie. She is brown as a berry now and Ronald says I am the best cook in the world. Well Jake all my love to you. There's a good time coming. So cheerio.

Mother x x

23rd June 1942

Airgraph

Dear John,

Just to let you know I have sent off your money today, 23rd June from Cooks Agency in Edinburgh so it should be in good time for your leave. At Cairo they will either send it on or ask you to call for it. See and have a good time wisely with it. I feel the better of the change here, Helen and Betty also. Nan is keeping house for me.

Lord Reek is having his teeth in this week. Can you picture him. Hope he disnae let them fall in his beer. Jean is not in the land army yet. Dr. Brand thought she should have a rest before starting so he knows best. Well John we are setting out to the zoo today. Hope they don't put us in a cage. Best of luck to you and let us hope you will be home ere long.

Love and kisses from mother x x x

Two of my father's mates at the tented camp in Heliopolis.

21ˢᵗ July 1942

Airgraph

Dear John,

Your air graphs coming through fine. I have sent away 2 lots of snaps. You may have gotten them by this. This is Glasgow Fair and pop was asking if I had put a card on the gate saying 'House Full'. I had soldiers in the hut at the weekend, London chaps. They want to come regular whenever they get a weekend pass. They are billeted at Stewarton so the top flat at home was, well you can picture it. Willie was among the crowd as Jean had taken 2 girls for the weekend. But the fun was good. Pop was saying we just need the sirens to go.

Do hope you keep fit John. You'll get a good holiday when this is all over. I'll see that the red book can take it. We are all well. The smallpox has broken out in Glasgow but it is now checked. Pop has written you in my last letter. You'll get a laugh. We all think a lot about you John. May the guardian angels keep watch over you. All my love to you.

Mother x x

Again, no evidence of the year posted but it appears that there was an outbreak of smallpox in Glasgow in 1942.

The 'red book' was where my grandmother kept details of all her income from letting rooms so that would be where she got the money to treat John to a holiday once the war was over.

Stewarton, about 20 miles north west from Ayr, became an army base in 1941 the main one being at Lainshaw estate. During the next few years various regiments and sections of the army were stationed there, including the Lancers, the Royal Engineers, the Rifle Brigade and the Lothian and Border Horse. Being so close to Ayr it was obviously a popular place for soldiers to visit.

There was also an army training site in the grounds of Craigie House which wasn't far from Lothian Rd.

24th August 1942

Airgraph

Dear John,

Mother calling, all well at home. Received your air mail letters with the lovely snaps. Lovely places. Willie also got his. David gets leave 11th September. You will be saying lucky chap. I am still busy but September will finish it. We have plenty of plums on the trees this year. Wish you were here eating them.

Hope you are keeping well. I think you look stouter in your snaps. We are all wearying for this war to end and you boys to be safe home again. Sad news about the Duke of Kent. No respect of persons. His wife will be so sad.

Hello John, Helen calling. We are going to the shore today with Roxie and Nan. We have not had much summer but the last 2 days have been good so are making the most of them. Will try and get photos taken as you suggest. Will be writing you a long letter soon. Lots of love.

Helen, Betty and mother x x

No year on date on the airgraph but due to the mention of Duke of Kent's death have placed it as 1942.

He was the fourth son of King George V. The duke and 14 others took off in a RAF Short Sunderland flying boat from Invergordon in Ross and Cromarty, to fly to Iceland.. The aircraft crashed on Eagle's Rock, a hillside near Dunbeath, Caithness.. The duke and all but one of those on board were killed. He was 39 years old.

September 8th 1942

Airgraph

My dear John,

Just received your photo this morning. It is splendid. Yes your look that seems to ask, 'What's cooking?'. We were all pleased to get it.

We have old Mrs Campbell from Strathaven staying for a holiday with us. She is 92 years of age and is going to town with me as smart as you like. She does not care a herrin heid* fur naebody.* What a character. Pop and her go away back to the old days at Strathaven.

Sorry if you lose your pal 'Porkie'. John Stewart the baker died last week. He took a heart attack at his work and died next day. John their son is away overseas, they did not know his destination so poor chap will not know yet. All well at home. Had a good season. Nan and I have sent a little cash for your Xmas. Let's hope we will all be together before another. Best wishes and love from everybody at home.

Mother x x x

Regarding the loss of 'Porkie' it is unclear if he was being transferred from my father's unit or had been hurt and would possibly die.

27th September 1942

Airgraph

My dear John,

Mother calling and sending you her love and best wishes. Hope you are well. David has gone back after his leave. He had a chap from his billet for a few days. He comes from Cumnock. The leave passed all too soon. The model he made me is lovely John. Mr Ogilvie's wife is now working in the food office. That will please him. Pop was at the shore on Saturday morning, he would likely be looking for a girl when who appeared but Nan, Roxie and Ronald, then Jean, Willie and their two so he had to spend the morning playing with his grandchildren. That would put his gas in a peep as old Jenny would say. Very busy this weekend, 4 rooms booked. Mrs Kerr is asking for you. I am writing Ivy today. All our love to you.

Mother x

In January 1940 the British government had introduced food rationing. Its aim was to ensure the population shared food equally at a time of shortages. Everyone was given a ration book with coupons and were needed to obtain rationed goods. Basics like sugar, meat, fats and cheese were some of the rationed items.

Eggs and butter were hard to get, only one egg being issued to each adult person in a week and 2 for children.

Fruit was almost non-existent but not rationed. On very rare occasions a greengrocer obtained some queues would form in the hope of getting an orange or a banana.

Food offices were where ration books were issued. Each person in the family had a registration number and people had an identity card which carried that number. That always had to be produced when new ration books were issued. Originally, they lasted for six months but towards the end of the war were extended to a year to cut down on administration. Coupons were taken to the place people were registered. Each coupon was marked with a week, and they would be cut out when the customer got their ration.

30th November 1942

Airgraph

My dear John,

Mother calling to you. Received your airgraphs and letters. You will be working very hard these days. Remember Johnnie Allen. He has died. He had very little blood and had 5 transfusions but it was no use. He was married. I think David is going to manage home at New Year. We will be thinking of you and wishing you were among us. See and be good to yourself. Spend all your money on good food. Father got a diploma for his war time exhibition loaf. Still to the fore. Wee David is 2 today. I hope you will be in good old Ayr for his next. Nan was over and stayed the night. We were all in the garden working on Saturday morning. I was the boss of course. Billy Gibson is way now in the merchant navy. His pop was not too pleased with him. All well at home.

All my love mother x x

ROYAL AIR FORCE
STATION.
HELIOPOLIS
CHRISTMAS DINNER 1942

The Commanding Officer Wishes
Every One
"A HAPPY CHRISTMAS"

MENU

CREME of TOMATO SOUP

FRIED LEMON SOLE

PARSLEY BUTTER SAUCE

STUFFED ROAST TURKEY

ROAST PORK APPLE SAUCE

ROAST POTATOES

GREEN PEAS CAULIFLOWER

XMAS PUDDING BRANDY SAUCE

CHEESE BISCUITS

FRESH FRUIT NUTS

BEER LEMONADE CIGARETTES

There may have been a war going on but appears that John had an excellent Christmas dinner.

1943

11th January 1943

Airgraph

Dear John,

A Happy New Year to you. Hope it will be good for us all. David has gone back, leave is over for this time. We had a very quiet New Year and all remained sober. David is looking well, a bit stouter, he does like getting home. Betty was 1st this term so is staying on at school. The ship Billy Gibson was on was torpedoed but he is safe. Quite an experience for Billy on his first trip. We are all well at home and plodding on as usual, wearying on the day when peace will be with us. I trust you are well son, and happy. We think of you every day and hope you will be back home soon. Keep your chin up and all our love to you.

Mother x

It did not take long for Billy Gibson to experience the dangers of being in the Merchant Navy. He had joined in November 1942 and his ship had been torpedoed early in January. It may be that he was a relation in some way as Nellie's maiden name was Gibson.

During World War II, the British Merchant Navy played a crucial role in keeping the United Kingdom supplied with essential materials. Approximately 144,000 merchant seamen served aboard British-registered merchant ships at the outbreak of the war, and up to 185,000 men served during the war. Casualties were high, with 25% of all crewmen killed or reported as missing.

January 1943

Airmail

My dear John,

Another note from the old homestead. This is the first air letter I have written, I see by the paper they are next best to the air graph. And how is the world using you these days. Good I hope.

Nan is sending you Roxie's photo in a box. Girl in Post office said that would be best. I was away at Kilmarnock yesterday seeing Mrs McKerrow, she had not been very well. Andrew was called up too. He will enlist in the Royal Artillery. We are sick to death of this dreadful war, can't get peace to live our lives as we would want.

Things are quiet at Ayr and the weather is awful, rain, rain every day. I am beside the fire a lot. Sewing and day dreaming. No word from Bill yet, Nan was over yesterday. Miss Roxie was like a blawn* rose. John and her daddy are coming home in a big boat, we hear that every day from her, she's a smarter. Bill is missing seeing her at her nicest age.

Well John news is scarce. I hope this finds you swinging along, singing a song. I saw Kenneth on Sunday, still as quiet. Aggie is getting yon wee back room made into a scullery. The woman is full of ideas. The place was fine the way it was. Does not know what to be at next. Well John all the best to you and all our love.

Mother x

Nan, Ronald and Roxie in the 50s   *Roxie with her grandma*

26th January 1943

Airmail

Dear John,

Just another wee note. You are nearing your 23rd birthday so let me here wish you many happy returns of the day. I can just picture you as the nurse handed you into my arms for the first time. A little bit of heaven right enough and the years rolled on bringing us this big stumbling block, the war.

Willie and I were sitting by the fire last night recalling the time you, Billy Gilchrist and he went to Croy shore to camp, leaving the bag in the bus and walking to the place, then heavy rain and the tent being put up. The 3 of you lying huddled together for heat and towels round your heads. Eventually you all went to sleep and wakened to the sun shining. Do you remember it? Maybe Jake you and I will have a car and a trailer and go camping. We'll take all the grand children with us.

Hope you are keeping well and that you have managed a little holiday. Hope you got the money alright. We are all well at home. Pop got his top teeth out. He is like one of you guys with the pipes in their mouths at shows. I'll have to sum up the courage to give him a kiss now.

Love John to you. Mother x x

Croy beach lies about 10 miles of Ayr near the village of Maybole.

9th February 1943

Air graph

Dear John.

A few lines as usual. Hope everything is going well with you. We are all well at home and plodding on as usual. The snowdrops and crocuses are in bloom telling us that spring is on the way.

I met Jessie Smith. She was saying John is not keeping well at all. He is in hospital down in Liverpool. I think he was training as a wireless operator. Mrs Smith with all her money can't buy health for her family. Jim Johnstone is away over soon. Jean's boyfriend is away also. He is in North Africa.

Frances Haines is now married. Her husband has a nursery. I expect in due season Frances will be starting one also. Ha. Ha. Well John I am weary waiting for the war to draw to a close. I am thinking of keeping a few hens at the back door. Don't you think it would be a swell idea. Suit faither getting them champed up in a cup. Well all the best to you my boy and all my love.

Mother x

Hello John. I'm in from school so send you all my love. Betty x

I presume from this letter that the Jean mentioned is Nellie's daughter. She did have an American boyfriend who was from Texas who she met

when he was serving with the USAF at Prestwick. They married before the war was over.

The nursery was situated near the town of Dumbarton.

1st March 1943

Airmail

Dear John,

Pop calling. Pleased to see by your letters that you are in good spirits and keeping well. You seem to have more time than I have for writing John. It's a case of a good day's work, a meal and into bed. I am up every morning at 2.30am, starting at 3.30 and home about 2.30 in the afternoon. Well when the weather is bad one can only go to bed. But now that the sun is beginning to shine.

Willie is making out a list of jobs. The latest brain wave he has had is for me to get a hen house built. So I am racking my brains drawing out the plans. He says we will start with about 4 hens or wondering if they will need a cockerel. Just like a woman I heard about that was having a problem in the same way. She sent her husband over to a neighbouring farm for 20 hens and 20 cocks. The farmer said go back and tell her there was no need for 20 cocks but she would insist. So the farmer came over and saw her himself and said what is your idea for having 20 cocks. Well she says I know well what it was to go short myself.

Well John it would be nice when you come home and mother could go out and bring you two nice fresh laid eggs. I was at Annbank on Saturday seeing them play a cup tie with Kirkintilloch Rob Roy. They got beat 4-2. I enjoyed the outing not having seen a match for a long time.

I am very busy in the bakery getting great praise for the bread I am turning out. This flour seems to baffle a lot of them. I had good experience of baking with it in the last war. Willie is down with tonsilitis. The doctor said it was touch or go of being diphtheria. Here's hoping he will make a good recovery as I like him being beside me, I think mother is a little better. I think as time goes on and the weather gets better she will be ordering us all about. 'Hey you. Will you get out to that hut or talk less, the dinner's ready, there's plenty hasn't got the likes you big wastrel, I laugh see? I would knock your face off.' True love John. Never mind John this good lord bless and keep her well for us all. Well John I hope this finds you well.

Cheerio, Dad.

Kirkintilloch Rob Roy and Annbank are two Junior Soccer teams. In that year Kirkintilloch won the Scottish Junior Football Cup so perhaps it is not surprising pop saw them win.

John and friend with a repaired Kittyhawk.

5ᵗʰ March 1943

Airmail

Dear John,

Just a line from the auld toon. Glad you are receiving some of our letters. I sent a £1 PO in one. I wonder if you got that. I have Miss Roxie with me today as Nan is away down town buying a dress for a wedding she is going to in March, a cousin of Bill's.

I am saying to Roxie just now that her grandpa is a scunner. She is saying he is not. Good grandpa. The tatties are getting wasted waiting on him. Standing blethering his head off to somebody. Glad you are having some leave. The post master general has started making enquiries about the money. Some guy will have stuck to the registered letters. I expect they will refund part of it.

David said that at Xmas they had a number of registered letters stolen and they never found out who did it. I thought the RAF was above that sort of thing.

Willie was off this week with tonsilitis but he is feeling okay now. Pop was saying I was feeling better, you are not to be thinking I was ill. You know the spring feeling, needing a tonic so have got one. Once I get these hens and get a few guid eggs over my neck I'll be ok. We are all missing the good things we used to get, butter etc. Well we were too well off and did not know it.

I saw big Tony the other day, he looks none too well. A life like yours would do him good. You seem to be having swell times, a lot you will have to tell us about.

Well John I'll need to sign off and get to town. The buses have stopped our way. All turn at the station now, saving petrol. Do you mind the day you were running after one at Boot's store. Made a hole in your waterproof. Aye and might have been hurt. Well all my love to you and be of good cheer.

Mother x x

It seems strange that my grandmother is remarking that my father is having a swell time even though there is a war going on. It certainly seems my father was able to sightsee and was far from the dangers of the front line. He visited many holy places in Jerusalem, visited the pyramids and swam in the Mediterranean.

However, I do know that on one occasion his base was bombed by Stukas but apart from that he did not seem to have endured any real hardships or danger although I do know he saw some bad plane crashes when damaged aircraft were trying to land.

Grandma and Grandpop White

13ᵗʰ March 1943

Airmail

Dear John,

Have just received an air mail letter from you dated 17ᵗʰ November and as you see it is the middle of March, so that took some time to come. It had 2 snaps in it with you and your chums. We thought you were looking well in it, a real smart guy and the best looking. Well you are at Alex. I'll bet you are enjoying the change. You were telling me about getting your tea and deciding it was not worth paying for and you and Parky making a hurried exit. You are like your mother, grudge paying for some thing that is not good.

Now I want to ask you did you receive a £1 postal order from Mrs Caddell at Xmas as you never said in your letters, so you might write her if you received it. Also sent you a £1 postal order in a letter. Did you get it? Let me know as I don't feel like sending them if you are not getting them.

This is a glorious Saturday morning so your ma is stepping out to town. I have got a lovely green hat and new shoes so I'll be feeling like a million dollars swanking along Ashgrove St. I am trying to get a hen hoose* and a chap has promised me some good laying hens so I am turning land girl. Aye but it's in ma ain gairden.* The chap I saw is a prisoner of war I see in today's post. His mother will be quite relieved as she thought he was dead. The mail is starting to arrive for the letting.

Well I am not giving attendance this year, they can get the rooms and cook for themselves. Quite a lot of people like it that way as they can come in when they like. Yours truly will be at the shore or perhaps dining at the Monument. Ha. Ha.

I'll need to be getting the camera on the go with some snaps for you. You have £50 to your name so I will see how I can get it soaring this summer. David has the same. He says we must get a car when you come back. Well we sure have room for a garage at the side of the house.

Good morning John, the sun is shining so mother and I are off to town. My exams at school are nearly finished now and thank goodness for that. Well John I'll say cheerio and all my love to you. *(Addition to the letter from John's sister.)*

Mother and Betty x x

The comment about the Italian prisoner of war is interesting. In Scotland most prisoners were judged to be a low security risk and enjoyed a considerable degree of freedom, many being allowed out of their camps to work on local farms, and their happy-go-lucky nature quickly endeared them to the Scottish public. However not all Italian POWs in Scotland were classed as harmless and free to work. Some were committed fascists, who even after Italy's surrender in September 1943 continued to support Mussolini. On December 15ᵗʰ, 1944, at a POW camp called Camp 14 in the Doonfoot area of Ayr 96 soldiers and an officer escaped through a tunnel. It appears that the soil was soft and easy to dig through. It was the largest mass escape of prisoners in Britain during the war.

The officer involved in the escape bid was called Lieutenant Pietro Graff, a 43-year-old officer in Italy's elite parachute division. Despite their attempt all the escapees were rounded up over the next few days and sent back to the camp. One group was spotted as they lit a fire in the woods to try and keep warm in the middle of winter. 4 escapees made it as far as Newton Mearns, 30 miles from Doonfoot.

The Alex mentioned is Alexandria, the second largest city in Egypt. It lies around 142 miles from Heliopolis where John was stationed.

Taken over Heliopolis by John on a test flight on a Liberator Bomber.

17th April 1943

Airmail

Dear John,

Is it not time for a few lines from home? I think so. All is well here, all are jogging along as usual. Monday is the spring holiday and we are all going to Strathaven on Sunday morning and staying till Monday night so we are hoping the weather will be good. Auld Jenny and I will have a good blether by the fire. Somebody's ears will be wringing maybe.

Willie is just in, he had been away a hike to Croy Bay with another chap. He said it was lovely. Does him good after being shut in the bakery. David is away back after his week's leave. He has two stripes on his arm, not bad John. And how is my young son. Keeping well and happy I hope. My but we're getting awfie* sick of this war. When is it going to end? I wish you were all home again and settled down. We have not got the hens. I think in the winters' days I would not be bothered with them. Too many eggs make you bilious anyway. Well John I will say cheerio for the present as Betty wishes to add a few lines. I send you all my love and I think of you all the time.

Dear John,

This is Betty calling. I've just got my holidays from school just now so will be able to give mother a hand. You can imagine her shouting at me, 'Whit are you looking' at noo.* Wasting time as usual.' Ha! Ha! As mother's told you we are going to Strathaven so I am looking forward to it. All the grandchildren are keeping well and getting big. And how's my big brother getting on these days? In the pink I hope. Well John I was second in the class this term. The girl who was first beat me by 1 and a half marks but luckily I've beat her in the first term so in the third term I'm afraid I'll have to watch my step. 'What say you?' Vicky's still the same old guy and still jogging along. Miss Kennedy in Boots was asking me how you were getting on. She is very good at giving us things that are scarce and that one cannot get without being in the 'know'. You boys are doing a good job out there so thumbs up. Your mate looks a very nice boy so tell him I was asking for him. Well John I will close.

Lots of love, Betty x x x

PS Helen is just finished checking up on my punctuations.

I suspect Vicky was the family dog and obviously all the plans for hens in the garden did not come to fruition.

The dog at my father's feet is possibly Vicky.

21st April 1943

Airmail

Dear John,

Just a wee note while I am at Strathaven. I am up here for a few days holiday as Betty has the Easter holidays and is able to run the house for me. She can tell pop where to get aff * and boss them all. Some girl.

The weather is lovely and I sure am enjoying myself. Betty, Helen and pop came with me on the Sunday and waited over till Monday night as Monday was Ayr Spring Holiday. We went to Stonehouse on the Sunday.

Pop was singing to you again. What a picture, nae teeth in. The wee boy was in fits laughing.

I hope you are well John. I sure am wearying to see you. I will hardly know you. Let's hope it won't be long. Nan has no word of Bill yet. He must be very sad at times thinking of her and the children. Won't we be all glad when it is over. I am writing this up in auld Jenny's and I am waiting for her son-in-law to come to the door with a pony and trap to take me a drive. Won't I enjoy it. It is a lovely day. I'll be writing you when I get home. I have people coming for the weekend. It is Glasgow spring holiday. That will be the start off for another season's letting. You will want the place to yourselves. Well John I have no more news so hope this finds you well. The heat will be starting out there, see and look after yourself well. All my love to you and may God keep you safe and happy

Mother x x

This is my birthday John, just 53.

Stonehouse is a small town around 35 miles from Ayr and just lying south east of Glasgow. It is only a few miles from Strathaven where my grandmother often went.

3rd May 1943

Airgraph

Dear John,

Just to let you know that Nan has had official word that Bill is a prisoner of war in Japanese hands so Nan is quite relieved that he is still in the land of the living. Sorry I have let the writing slip. Cleaning and you know what that means. Glad to say we are finished and the home looks nice and fresh.

We had the Stonehouse full for the weekend. The weather was beautiful and they enjoyed themselves to the full. Pop was dressed up and the fun was good..

Hope you are well John. I've turned down the hen idea, on a wet day I would not fancy them all standing around on my leg. I think I'll prefer a swanky hut in the corner. Just went to the door. Postie with an air mail letter from you. Yes all the garden is done, wish I saw you in that deckchair. A roast chicken in the oven. Those days will come so keep hoping.

Love mother x x

4ᵗʰ June 1943

Airgraph

Dear John,

Received an airgraph this morning so you know about poor Victor, just remember all is for the best. I think I hear him laughing yet. The weather is glorious. I have sent you a lot of snaps. Pop and I are going for a week's holiday, a rest we will take at Strathaven.

Jean has been discharged rom the army. She had a nervous breakdown but is home and working in a confectioner's shop in Alloway. She is very well now and so glad to be home. 'It's an ill wind that blaws naebody guid.' I get her pay now. I am all booked up for the summer so am quite pleased. Well John we think of you always. Try and keep well. Surely it will end soon. Boots send their regards.

All my love to you.

Mother x

26th June 1943

Airgraph

Dear John,

Received your letter dated April 2nd you will see this is June 26th, closing day. Betty was first in her class and first in Bible. She looked very smart in her new costume. I used to go and look at you on closing day. Expecting David on leave on the 6th July for a week. We will get more snaps taken and send them on. The heat must be very trying at times for you. I do hope you will keep well. All busy at Ayr. Nan sent you a greetings telegram. Emma Ogilvie won the Burns' prize for singing. She was not too good, excited I think. Jean got your letter, she is at home now, got her discharge. She is very glad she is beneath the lights of home now. She is out at business. Well John all my love to you, had your red book down to the bank today. You can now start singing, 'Higher still and higher.'

Love Mother x

I think Nan's discharge was on health grounds from some part of the armed forces.

14th July 1943

Airgraph

Dear John,

Received one of your long letters this week. Pleased at all you say. David is at home at present and enjoying the rest. H & B have gone to Straiton for a week. Ronald is there also, I bet they are enjoying themselves.

We hear that the names of prisoners of war are on their way to this country, so expect news of Bill soon. Let's hope it will be good. All well at home. Kenneth sends you his best wishes.

We have to get permits for visitors to Ayr now. Having quite a good time to myself since the No Attendance order has come into force – move over Nellie!

Hi ya John, David calling, having a grand time, sorry to say I go back tomorrow. Just been hearing an RAF C.O. from Cairo speaking about the great work the ground staff are doing, so keep it up Jake and we'll be seeing you soon.

David and mother

There is no year stamped on the air gram but due to the reference about Bill I think this was sent in 1943 but can't be certain.

I am uncertain what the 'No Attendance' order meant as my research has found no mention of this..

John is second from the left

19th July 1943

Airgraph

Dear John,

Here we are again and it's Glasgow Fair. The town is very busy with visitors. Yes you are right about terms. We sure know how to charge and do see we get it. This year it is £3 per week per room. Nae bother at aw. Have you received the £7 I sent from Edinburgh. Have they a place in Cairo you could call and ask. They told me in Edinburgh that they had.

I have a young man from Stonehouse staying here. He is your double. I just think it's you. The weather here is warm. You will be saying we should be with you. Trust you are well and have a nice holiday. Love from all at home.

Mother x x x

The £3 per room in 1943 for a week's stay would equate to £134 today, still good value for money.

7th August 1943

Airgraph

Dear John,

Received your cablegram today. Glad you got money. Just heard from David that he is to proceed to Morecombe so I am afraid he will be going abroad. He had leave but was at his girl's place so don't expect he will manage home. I don't like these farewell visits anyway. I'm sick of this war. Any day now would suit me for it to finish but will it?

We are all well at home. Pop has got his teeth now. I believe people would be willing to pay 1/- to see him eating. Hope you are well and looking after yourself. I have been very busy as usual this year but managed good wee jaunts between times. Do you see only green in ma een?* Well all for the present son and all our love to you from the old homestead.

Mother x x

I have been told that David's girl's parents were very wary of him at first as he was a Scotsman. She was from a Suffolk town called Clare.

20ᵗʰ August 1943

Airgraph

Dear John,

Here we are again, getting all your mail fine. You are just the same gay John as your letters denote. I have sent you £1 postal order, hope you get it. Have a good meal. All well at home. Got a letter or two from David. He is in India, Bombay I think. I had a weekend at Strathaven. Went to Stonehouse also. All asking for you. I have got the big corner at the bottom of the garden concreted, all ready for posh hut I mean to have. It will be ideal for quietness, unless when the birds begin in spring mornings, anyway I would like it to be ready for you boys when you come home. Jean is fine now, got a light job at Gilchrist's , quite a good pay. J.G. has been liberal. Helen is making good progress, has had an increase also. Betty is going to be at home for winter. She will go out in the spring.

Love from all here. Mother x x x

The G in J.G. must stand for a member of the Gilchrist family who owned the bakery.

Betty, Helen and Joyce (David's girl)

28th August 1943

Airgraph

Dear John,

Mother calling. How is my son these days? David has gone overseas. Willie went down south to see him off. He is now engaged to Joyce. What were you saying about a wee girl back home? John you had better be a gay bachelor for a while, have a good time at home.

I was away at Hamilton yesterday. Successful landladies always take a day off to preen themselves. David was hoping he would land out beside you. We are all well. I am losing a lot of fat so am quite pleased. I am very busy, did well this year. Money for old boots John. Easy made. A dash of personality works wonders. I study each batch and play up to them. All the grand children are ok. I love them all. Well thumbs up old boy.

Love from mother x x

David did not end up in Egypt but sent even further east, to India and was stationed near the Indian city of Bombay. My cousin still has a gift he brought home from there for Nellie.

1st September 1943

Airgraph

Dear John,.

Just received a letter from you so here's a line in return. This is 1st September. It's raining buckets. Am still busy letting, booked for September. I prefer the busy life, keeping the mind occupied is the finest tonic I know. We are all well. Willie has had his medical. He is going down this week for an interview for the navy. Trying to get in at his trade. So you are all getting ripped in. Wish it was over. Billy Gilchrist is missing. Remember the camping days. Mr Millar was asking for you

Photo in uniform if possible for the Toc H room. I don't have one. Try and get them taken and send him one.

Pop's hut is now fitted with electric light. Good going. Some of the profits did that. Remember the night you arrived home and we were all parked in it. What a yell of delight when we saw your face.

Love from all at home. Mother x x

No further mention is made of Willie's attempt to join the navy but from future letters it is obvious that he was not accepted as his employment changes during the following years..

A formal picture of John in dress uniform.

4th September 1943

Airmail

Dear John

A few lines from the auld toon. We are now into September and the weather has been very bad lately. You would have had an air graph from Jean, I saw her writing to you. She was telling you about being in hospital. Well you need not be alarmed as Dr Brand said she would need complete rest and quiet. The munitions factory has been too much for her. The long hours and strain. So I sent her to a nursing home. It cost me 3 guineas a week. She had 2 months in it but is home now and feeling fine. She will be exempt from war work. Mrs Gilchrist is giving her a light job in the store packing cakes etc along with Mrs Simpson the lady who stays with me. She is a young person. Her husband is in the Scotia camp at Doonfoot. She has my first bedroom and has been with me for a year now. Her and I get on fine, never a word all the time, always giving me a wee hand about the scullery , so Jean will be fine with her going to work together and coming home together.

They start at 6 o'clock and finish at 3 o'clock. Our Jean's nerves can't stand noise and the banging of the machinery so thought I had better explain. She matters to you. I never told you in case you would be worried. Well Betty has left school.

A letter has come from Mr Lockhead the master of the Grammar offering her a job as clerkess. The school education authority have asked him to engage a girl so he has given Betty the first chance. She has to learn typing and shorthand at school in the evening. So Betty starts out on a career. Believe me John there are no flies on her.

I have had a busy year. The drawings reached the three figure mark, no bad for a dunner heid* like your mother. *Dyes Fyrie*?? has got the order for an outside lavatory so Lothian Rd. still flourishes. Time marches on and so for the present goodbye.

Love mother x x

The building of an outside lavatory seems strange as I am sure they would have had an indoor one. The house does not look huge but as can be seen lodgers were taken in as well as my grandmother and grandfather and their daughters Helen, Jean and Betty who were at home at this time.

The Scotia Camp had been built by Billy Butlin, the holiday camp entrepreneur, after the navy asked him to build two camps for their use. One was built in North Wales and one to the south of Ayr, not far from the Italian Prisoner of war camp. In the planning of the camp Mr Butlin was thinking of its use as a holiday venue when the war was over which in fact it became and which I actually worked at in the summer of 1970 washing dishes.

The cost of Jean's rest home for her stay in today's money values would be around £950. It does seem rather confusing as to Jean's timeline. The letters have not indicated when she started working in the munition's factory which may have been situated at a place in Ayrshire called Ardeer.

On back of photo sent home

'A native street scene. Cairo 1943 How would you like some of that fruit?'

22nd September 1943

Airmail

Dear John,

Just to let you know we received your letter with the photograph of you and all the snaps. We all think you are looking grand. The life oot* there hasnae* kilt* you. What a wonderful place the holy land is. I think the big majority of folk in the world today forget about the nails and the cross. You will have a lot to tell us when you come home. I wish it was next week.

We are all well and jogging along as usual. Jean is fine now. Got a good job in Gilchrist's checking boards and the vans. I am still busy, the season has been a long one, never mind this is a grand sideline. I can make a better pay than your father. My drawings reached the three figures this year. Of course I have expenses. £40 for Jean's treatment, a set of jaw clappers for old blowhard, £15. I asked him if he could just have a few of them inset with gold, made them a bit dearer.

I told you we have the light in the hut. It's a real bonus, an electric heater also. I can just march in, switch on the light, walk up to David's bedside and tell him a few home truths occasionally, then breeze out and snap out the light. Leave him alone with his thoughts. Ha. Ha. Nevertheless he thinks I am the cleverest woman in Ayr. What I tell him is yer* no clever, nor smart, I could buy and sell you at the first corner. Well he is leading a very quiet life and we are getting along fine. Drink in the pubs is scarce, no whisky on Saturdays, only beer. I think that was done for the American soldiers as they could not stand the Scotch stuff so it is as well for them all.

We all think you are looking well. I wonder how David is faring. Heart broken nae doot* being awa* frae* Joyce. That will be a wedding when the war is over. You take my advice my boy and be a bachelor for a long while yet. I'll aim at a car and we'll have some good times. Well John this is Friday and a lot of business to be done so I'll get cracking so cheerio and keep smiling.

Love from mother x x

Pop on the left won many awards for his bread making. In this picture he was on his way to London to receive such an award. The year is uncertain.

27th November 1943

Airgraph

Dear John,

How are you. Well I trust. We are getting near the end of the year so send you Xmas greetings. Hope you have a pleasant one. Surely you will sit in the old home for next Xmas dinner. I'll have a turkey that day sure enough not to mention the Xmas pudding. All goes well at home. I've 2 rooms let permanently and get on well with the people. It's company also. The best of it all I'm the landlady Ha. Ha. Nae bother a taw. Collecting the dough with a smile and a song. Hope you get the snaps ok. Only ones we had taken this year. David is feeling the heat, he will be getting brown. You both will.

Love from mother

John

1944

29th January 1944

Airmail

Dear John,

Just received 28th January your letter dated January 17th, so that's quick work coming, matter of 10 days. I have sent you a registered letter with a P.O. for £1. I guess you can use it Jake. We are all wondering if you could send us almonds. Let us know in your next Air G and we will send on money for some. News this week is that Mr Wells the saddler was killed. He had an accident and was seriously injured and died that same evening. It is his daughter that is learning Betty the piano so one never knows what is round the corner in this life. Willie is at the back door now making a big coal box for himself, gets more peace to work here than at Victoria Rd. Then he will get one of the vans to take it over. Very cold here last week. I am wearying for those warm summer days then I'll get off my mask to bask in it. Won't you boys be needing a good rest when you get home? No fleeing awa tae* anither* job for a while, just can be gentlemen of leisure. It will be all one a hundred years after this.

Nan had 2 postcards from Bill. In last night's papers they were gravely concerned about the treatment the Japs are dishing out to P.O.W.s. Let's hope Bill is not too badly off. My I'm sick of that bally war for one and there are many like me.

Dr. Forgan got your letter. Mrs Forgan is very ill yet. Miss Alice is standing by now. I've to send you kisses, here they are, she will make them herself. *(At this point there are several X marks.)* She says it is awful writing and I am telling her it sure is. Well John, nothing new, all sliding along as usual. In a few months the letting will begin and the handbag gets a bit heavier. I'm getting my lugs* back for the big bonus.

Pop will likely be sending you something. Gets it in March he thinks. I've a great notion for a holiday in the country and I'll be seeing I get it. Had a visit of Frances. She is married now to a chap who has a nursery, vegetables and flowers I mean you know. She looks very well, takes life very easy and gets away with it. Cheerio for present. Mind you are to be a bachelor for a long time.

Love from mother x x

Alice mentioned is my cousin and the second child of Willie and Jean. Mr Forgan was the minister at church Nellie attended.

14th February 1944

Airgraph

Dear John,

Received your last letter with all the news of your leave also snaps. What a wonderful time you had. No wonder you did not get our snaps. I sent 2 lots to David. Dunner heid*. I must have been dreaming. Well there is another lot on their way to you. Did you get cigarettes Aunt Caddell sent you. She got Mr English to send them. She wants to know. So write her an A.G. and tell her if you received them.

I hear David and Jim will be seeing each other soon. Craigie Avenue and Gordon Terrace will be in the news. Aunt Agnes of Dongola Rd. has to depart time nursing now, Ian is 14 now, a big braw lad., always laughing. Goes to Bible class. Betty says she can hardly keep from laughing watching him. 'Dr. Forgan says no bible class next Sunday' he says then shakes hands with himself , what a boy. Hope you are still on top of the world John and keeping merry. The sun is blazing on the airgraph. It will carry my blessing to you and all my fondest love.

Mother x x

John is on the right in front row

23rd March 1944

Airmail

Dear John,

Hello again. Getting your mail ok. Thanks John for your birthday greetings. Let's hope you are by my side by another birthday. Pop got your letter alright. He is still the same daft devil. Laughs at everything. We are working in the garden these days. Having a few alterations put in and it is looking very nice.

Did you ever get the snap Nan sent you? Hope I get the almonds you sent me soon. I'll be making nut buns. Don't you wish you were munching one. The news is strange about Billy Gilchrist. He is presumed killed now. My didn't you feel sad about him, a guid boy he was. I always liked him. Remember your camping days with him. Willie felt it very much. He is wearing a scarf that belonged to him. I will be writing about him to David. Mind the play he was in as the faither. Billy courting his daughter. We did not know we were well off then.

Willie has gone to Dunfermline for the training. He does not care for it but he is looking well. The change out the bake house is doing him good but you know Willie likes to be at home with the weans* and Jean. He tells me he gets some good laughs at the chaps. There are some hard boiled eggs among them. Helen and Betty are away at pictures tonight, 'Wuthering Heights.' I was there last night. I was greeting* at it. It was here 4 years ago, maybe you saw it. Betty had her first love letter today, some boy asker her to meet him at the Odeon. He hails from Old Toll I said add a y to it and tell him to run on. Whit a laugh we had. Betty says he has buck's teeth and can't spell. I told her she will have to stay with me for years and years. Friday is the day for the bonus to be dished out. I will be ready to grab the bulk of it.

Well John the Jerries are giving London a bit of a touch up again. When will it end? I have started spring cleaning. The letters are arriving in for the letting so the glass is rising now. Wait till you are lying in the deck chairs at the back door. That will be the day.

Love from mother x x

Willie was training to be a coal miner.. It may be that he was one of what was called 'Bevin's Boys'. They were young British men conscripted to work in coal mines between December 1943 and March 1948 to increase the rate of coal production, which had declined through the early years of World War II. The programme was named after Ernest Bevin, the Labour Party politician who was Minister of Labour and National Service in the wartime coalition government.

The men were chosen by lot with 10% of all male conscripts aged 18–25 selected for work in the mines. Many were upset at this as they wanted to fight while other were pleased as it meant not being involved at the front.

The 1944 attack on London was the last time the Germans bombed the city. It lasted from January to May 1944 and involved 474 German bombers, 379 of which were destroyed. It was nicknamed the 'baby Blitz' as it was so much smaller than the 1940-41 blitz. It achieved very little.

28th March 1944

Airmail

Dear John,

Received your parcel at long length and boy are we all delighted with the contents. Won't I be the lady posing along Ashgrove St. with the handbag and a little of the perfume on. The girls are enraptured with the stockings. Shapely legs are to be put into them John. Jean thinks the bag lovely. Well this is March as you see above and it is like summer here. As I write this pop is sweating like a race horse digging the garden. We have all been lending a hand and it is looking fine. I had a little wall built around the first rockery, brought it up to the level of the green so that when we look out from the living room window we see the flowers instead of it being on a slope. Much tidier and kept in order easier. Must have efficiency in this department. Pop was telling Nan (she was in the garden) the minute she sees me there is a dozen jobs on the go. What a woman for work. He had taken a great big clump of something out the garden. I was helping him to lift it to throw it over the wall. 'Dae ye ken* whit* grave this is fur*.' Nan was in fits at the pant. I could not lift for laughing.

So we wend through the days with laughter and sometimes tears. I am fully booked for Easter weekend and I have Mrs Kerr coming. She is having a week. She will be fine company for me and we will go out together. Leaves me free to have Betty to carry on at times. Might as well take a bit of leisure, all work and no play makes Nell a dull girl.

Willie has completed his course at Fife. He is being transferred to Glenburn Pits. He started at 7 o'clock in the morning. They have baths at Glenburn so he won't be coming home with a black face, a sad state of affairs, a chap with such artistic hands as Willie howking* coal. Och there's a war on. He is looking well though. The change from the bakery has done him good. He is not bothering, says it won't last and that he will be making a beeline after the war for a good job as a decorator. There is good money in that for him.

Well John there is no more news. This is Friday so I am going to town to get a bit of business done. I put £10 in your red book, same as David's. £20 in my own, that was off the bonus. Nan got £5, Willie £5, Helen, Betty and Jean the same. Ah well it is in safe keeping. A £1 is your best friend any day. I have no accounts, everything is paid on the dot. I like an easy mind and I am H.A.P.P.Y.. Love to you from everybody at home. Thanks for your lovely gifts.

Mother x x

Glenburn was situated near Prestwick so Willie would have been able to get to and from work easily as it was only around 5 miles from his home. His plans to be a decorator after the war did not come to fruition although strangely his third child, Billy, born 2 months after this letter did.

John setting off to work early in the morning.

24th April 1944

Airmail

Dear John,

Received your photo and snaps. Well we all think you look well, you are a bit stouter or is it you were near the camera. Still the same guid* looking boy but it would suit me better if you were dashing in the back door at night for your supper. I'm very tired of this war and all the disasters it has brought but there is no use grumbling, we have to see it finished.

Mrs Forgan died on Easter Sunday and my dear friend Mrs McKerrow passed away last week. She had been ailing for a long time and when Andrew was sent overseas it kind of finished her.

I received your greetings telegram for my birthday, I'm getting on, 54 if you didn't know. However you are just as old as you feel so some days I am only 20. I have invited Joyce for her holidays if she would like to come. The railways are not promising much these days, might be no holidays allowed. Willie was round last night, he is looking fine. Out of the bakery has helped him.

We got the almonds and raisins okay. The cooks were busy I'll say. I'm making a dumpling with the raisins. Wish you had a bit. Faither is in today laughing his sides sore at Red Snooks shop, a big sized suit, black tails, swears he is going in to try it on and keep it for funerals. He says auld* Dunlop wid* shut the gates if he saw him coming with it on. I tell you we do get the laughs.

He has two Italians working in the bakery and he is speaking like them. Bake a the tattie scones and the cook a the bread, you ought to hear him. Well John I'm sweating for the day you'll be tumbling out at Ayr Station. I'll hire the poshest car in Ayr for you. Keep well and I've nothing but happy memories of you. You were a good boy at all times so cheerio and keep smiling. All will be well yet.

Love from mother x x

I may have misread the bit about 'Red snooks' shop but the writing was difficult to decipher.

Italians working in the bakery alongside Pop is another example of Italian Prisoners of War being able to work in the community. I can certainly imagine my grandfather making fun of their accents.

18th May 1944

Air gram

Dear John,

I've got another grandson. Arrived on the 16th May. They are both well. He is being called William. We are lending a hand with Alice and David. Jean is in Dalblair Nursing Home. Nae sick* nonsense for us. A week or 10 days in bed then up and at it. I tell them I would not relive my life for the best man breathing. Well so I say.

Weather right cold here yet. David's girl is coming her holidays. We will try to get some snaps taken for you boys. Spools are scarce. Roxie was 4 this week. She got a pram and doll from the Cowans. You ought to see her, typical mother. I get many a laugh from my grandchildren. All my thoughts and love,

Mother x x

William was the third child of Willie and his wife Jean. He became known to us all in later years as Billy. The Cowans would have been Nan's husband's parents.

31st May 1944

Airmail

Dear John,

Hello boy a line or two. I missed writing last week as I had Alice and David over, while Jean was at nursing home. A little boy again. So once more the work begins, bathing, washing nappies, making bottles. What a work. I'm glad I've retired from that line of business. The one I am in is much more profitable. I see by your last letter you are going on leave. I won't have time hardly to send you anything but I'll post a little on and you'll get it after your leave as you will be skinned. I'll see what I can do.

The letting starts now so I'll be kept busy, just as well, keeps you from thinking too much. I'm going to be asking them well this year for plenty of dough. Nae use except I get big terms. Wee David was very good over here. I could keep him. I thought the clock had rolled back 21 years. He is so like you as a little boy. Jean is keeping fine. Willie will give her a good hand. He is a good chap. Let's hope she knows it. His heart is no in this pit business but he has just got to do it. My but the world is upside down, goodness knows when it will be right. I am very well John for which I am thankful and this wee hoose* is paradise to me. The hawthorn is out on the trees and the grass is so green. I would not change my surroundings for anything. I've got my private room ready, the hut, where I send out terms, count the cash and swear at your faither. Ayr is very busy now. We will see if McMillan can give us a film or two. Willie got one so you will be getting snaps as soon as we can get them developed. Ronald has a new suit, my but he is braw*. Lovely colour he has and very good teeth. We are into June tomorrow, time simply flies. I was away a run to Glasgow to see Francis. Betty was with me. Her husband has a nursery away past Dalmuir. We got a lot of plants for the garden. You will notice I combine business with pleasure.

Well John I send you all my love and am just wearying on that day when you'll be home with us

Love from all, mother x x x

'Wee David' was to become in later years a theatrical agent representing people like Hollywood star Danny Kaye and British actress Eleanor Bron.

12th June 1944

Airgraph

Dear John,

Another airgraph to say I got a letter this morning. I see your leave is in July. I sent you £5 by Cook's. It is just a little to help you along. Well the invasion has started, let us hope for good results. Joyce does not know whether she will manage through now as the trains might be off. Had a few snaps taken. I am posting them today so you can be on the look out for them. I am busy now so letters might not just be as regular. I like the letting. It is a cheery life and the dough is good. I bought a wee clock this week and they tell me it is just like myself, chimes the hours so quickly. They laugh they hear it. Aye well one has got to be on their toes tehse days. You have a speedy way yourself. Well John watch that stomach of yours.

Love from all. Mother x x

The invasion mentioned is the D-Day invasion which began on the 6th June 1944 and obviously lifted the spirits of the people and as Nellie said good results were being hoped for.

The next letter indicates that Joyce would be with Davd in Ayr at the end of July. There was rail travel disruption due to the D-Day landings. Railway restaurant cars were withdrawn from service on 5 April 1944. By the end of May 1944, 264,000 train miles were cut from the timetables as the tracks were cleared for Operation Overlord. Overcrowding on services remained until restrictions were relaxed that October.

Nellie outside 1 Lothian Rd.

2ⁿᵈ July 1944

Airgraph

Dear John,

A line from the old home. Had a letter from you today. Hope the wee boil has disappeared by now. Blood too rich eh!

We are now into June. The time seems to fly. We have got the old ledger going again. But mam has got wise to it and just ain't going to kill herself.

We will be having David and his girl with us on the 24ᵗʰ. My I wish the war was over and you were home again. I don't think I'll ken* ye. Everybody talks about Betty being so like you. Was in at Boots. Got a wee bottle of Evening in Annbank perfume from red head. She sends you her regards.

This is going to be a lovely day so yours truly is going out. Well John all my love to you. Keep fit and happy. Will send dough soon.

Mother x x

I presume Nellie is joking abut the name of the perfume. Annbank is a small village not far from Ayr.

5th July 1944

Airmail

Dear John,

A line or two from home. Joyce has gone home now after a very good holiday. I see she likes Ayr and got peace to sleep at night without the alarms. She looked fine going back. David would be wishing he was at Ayr. She is the very sensible type and I think she and David will be ok. Of course time will tell. Ayr is very busy now. We had snaps taken so yours will be on their way as soon as we get another lot developed. They are not so smart at these things now. Short staffed etc.

I hope you got the money ok John. I'll be giving the wee red book a leg up now that the leasing has started. I have very nice people just now, so kind to me with little extras.

I see the tomato growers at Stonehouse sent 300 lbs of tomatoes to the wounded soldiers. I was writing Willie Marshall Davie and wondering when the publicans would be sending out free beer tae drouthy* bakers. I was a run there last week. The countryside is lovely. Nan and I are going for a day with Ronald and Roxie so hope the sun will be shining.

Have you been on leave yet? You will fairly enjoy a change from work. If this war would end soon and you were home I would be happy.

The bakers are very busy now. Ayr is packed with visitors. They say don't travel but they forget folk must get a change or go crackers. Well John there is little to write about these days. Helen got the offer of a job at the Hannah Research at Auchencruive but her boss wanted to hold on to her. She got a 7/6 rise and Mr Bell said we do appreciate your services Miss White. No bad, that's £2-7-6 a week she has. I am getting a little more from Boots for you. There is a paper to fill in. I better send it on I expect. Aunt Caddell is still jogging along, not going to bother with summer visitors. I canna get enough, take them all. Season is not long in passing and the money is good.

Well John it's bed time. I'll say cheerio and take good care of yourself. Wait till you see the snaps. There is one that will make you laugh, papa and mama.

Love from mother x x

Based on inflation Helen would be receiving around £108 a week now.

The Hannah Research Institute where Helen was offered a job lies just outside of Ayr and studied aspects of dairy farming. During the war it investigated farm self-sufficiency, protein substitutes for dairy cows, bovine mastitis and the preparation and storage of dried milk.

Research was also undertaken on the bacteriology of evaporated and sweetened condensed milks and on problems related to canned cream. In 1943 the dehydration of foods, including vegetables, fish and milk, became increasingly important and the Institute was chosen to stage a demonstration to illustrate the value of modern methods of dehydration and their possible applications in the food industry.

A main street in Heliopolis

23rd July 1944

Airmail

Dear John,

I am getting behind with my letters but it is the Glasgow Fair and you know what that means. The town is crowded with visitors and the weather is lovely. I'm doing good business myself and find time to enjoy myself a bit also. A run on the bus looking at the countryside suits me.

I sent off snaps to you and I have other ones being developed and will send them off. They are very good. You'll get a laugh and your maw and paw. I also sent some papers from Boots for you to sign. I enclosed a postal order for you to get a treat. I had your red book down town, must add something from the Glasgow Fair drawings. Everybody does like staying here. Is it the hoose* or the wuman?* Aggie had 2 boarders who left her last week. She does too much grousing I fear.

The bombs are pretty bad at London. Children are being evacuated to the country. I hope aunt Bes will be okay always. I saw your snap up at Nan's. Bert and you, very good it is. Alice has got her tonsils out and is getting on ok.

Our Jean was up at Frances' place giving her a hand with plants and tomatoes. They have a nursery. I take a run there myself. It is near to Dumbarton. Milton they call it, very quiet place but a lot of traffic to Dumbarton and Helensburgh. He is a very nice chap that Frances married, real business. Neither smokes or drinks. All for his business and seems to love the life. I think Frances could get more of a hustle on. He is smart anyway, has a dozen greenhouses, big ones. Well John that is a place you can visit when you get home.

I hope you are well, surely the war is nearing an end. The plum and apple trees are laden. I can see a lot of happy bairns* in a little while wolfing into them. Wee David is a nice wee* soul. I pet them all a lot much to their liking believe me. If they are in tears I join them.

Love from mother x x x

As mentioned previously the Glasgow Fair was held annually in the first two weeks in July. Local businesses and factories closed on 'Fair Friday' to allow workers and their families to travel, typically spending their time in the Firth of Clyde or Ayrshire coast. This practice was known as going "doon the watter" ("down the water") in the Glasgow dialect. It was obviously a very busy and profitable time for my grandmother with letting rooms at the house.

The mention of bombings in London refers to the V1 rockets or doodlebugs as they were known, hitting the capital city. They started in June 1944, in answer to the D-Day landing in France a week earlier.

Approximately 10,000 were fired at England; 2,419 reached London, killing about 6,184 people and injuring 17,981. The greatest density of hits was received by Croydon, on the south-east fringe of London.

15th August 1944

Airmail

Dear John,

How are you. I've been falling behind with my mail. I've been galivanting this week. Was at Stonehouse for 2 days, took Alice with me. Then I was at Glasgow on the Saturday with pop. Then a day away with Nan so I can still get off my mark John. The country is looking it's best. Just received the snap and two big ones. You are looking fine. Sitting at the table wish the dinner was coming along and a fine bunch of lads in the other one. Pop says you are the best looking yin among them all. For once I did not disagree with him.

Had a letter from David this morning. He is well. He will be fed up with the heat, however he said that they had rain so that made a change. Ayr is still busy. I am finishing up end of August and going for a holiday by myself to Strathaven. The summer seems to fly by. We had a heat wave for a fortnight. You ought to have seen the shore John, black with people. Nan and I have been to Strathaven to look for a room. We intend spending a fortnight there so we are lucky and got one so you can picture us setting out. It will be a change of air and do us good. Trust the weather will be on its best behaviour. I wonder if this bally war will soon be over. One gets fed up thinking of it. Nothing seems kind of real these days.

A plane crashed on Prestwick shore and 5 Americans were killed. Ronald was all excited about it. He got the book you sent him. I saw your picture cooking your breakfast, only I am not left handed, she is. *(Presume this is in reference to something in the book.)* Just wish I was cracking in twa* guid* eggs for ye. Well here's hoping.

People at the door just now wanting the last fortnight in September but I said no. We will have settled down by then and the nights will be creeping in. Nothing new at home, all jogging along as usual. Betty will be starting work in the autumn. She has a notion to go into MacArthur's shop. She has no notion for the office life so we will have to cut that out. Well John I am waiting for pop to come in for his dinner so will close and se what's cooking. Trusting you are well and happy. It will be a great day when you arrive home, so let time march on. Nan has had no word from Bill since Xmas. I often wonder what he will be like. So cheerio John and love from all at home.

Mother x x

20th August 1944

Airgraph

Dear John,

Your mail arriving ok. Me, Jean, Nan, Ronald and Roxie are going off to Strathaven for a few days so here's to a guid holiday. I'll spend some of my drawings. Betty and Helen are invited to Greenock for a week. They go when we come back. Then we will settle down for the winter. Good news we are in Paris. Won't be long till you are home now.

We have a lot of the wounded arriving at Ayr, Americans. We watch them coming off the trains, stretcher cases.

Have you ever received a registered letter with Boots' papers and 30/-? Let me know as I sent it. I thought I sent a P.6?? address for it. Well hope you are well.

Ayr is not as busy now. A hint of autumn in the air. Will write you when on holiday. We are quite looking forward to the change.

Love from all. Mother x x

1st September 1944

Airmail

Dear John,

Here I am at Strathaven on a week's holiday. I'm kind of wearying and be glad to get back home so guess there is no place like home. However I have had a rest and change of air. Auld Jenny is still to the fore. What a woman at 93 years of age. She has been a smarter. She does her own washing and work yet. Helen and Betty are going for a week's holiday so we are all spending cash. Mind I would rather have it.

An American plane crashed at Beresland Rd, Prestwick just about a mile from the drome. Landed on top of bungalows. They were burned outright. Crew and 14 passengers all perished. *(Part of letter here indecipherable as written in pencil)*

Nan and Roxie were here last week and Jean. Jean and I had this week. We will get settled down for the winter now and another black out. When do you think you will be home John? We did not get the snaps away to you yet. *(Rest of section indecipherable then she uses a pen)*

I am home now John and quite glad. It has poured all day Sunday and the home is so quiet with Helen and Betty away. There is only pop, Jean and I. I am longing for you and David home John. The autumn days bring a kind of sadness with them. I was listening to Bing Crosbie singing, he is over here at present. You were asking about pyjamas. I'll need to send you on a pair. There are some in the loft. The plums are ripe now. The kids are enjoying them. Roxie is home now, her tonsils out. She is fine, a braw wee lassie*. Master David is a cute yin*. You ought to see his eyes when he talking and the hand going full of expression. Willie dotes on him, no wunner*. When he comes round it's 'How's Nellie'. Nothing new. Pop is reading by the fire, a lazy mawk* at writing.

(It appears at this point that 'pop' has been persuaded to write something to his son.)

Hello John, having a rest by the fire listening to the wireless. Everything seems to be going fine these days with the war. We are all looking forward to it being finished soon. Have had a very busy summer. Baked more bread than any previous years. Another fine gentleman in our line of business has passed on *(name indecipherable)* The bakery still goes on. Nellie has often said to me to take things easy as that is just what happens. She draws the insurance money and becomes a merry widow. *(Some more writing is squeezed in but indecipherable also. He finished with)*

All the best of luck, pop.

My grandmother mentions the air accident at Beresland Rd in Prestwick but reports at the time indicate it was at Hillside Avenue which is very close by. On Monday 28ᵗʰ 1944 a Douglas C-54 Skymaster from the United States Airforce crashed into the street while attempting to land at Prestwick airport in poor weather conditions. The crash claimed the lives of 6 crew members, 13 servicemen, a nurse travelling on the flight and 5 civilians.

9ᵗʰ September 1944

Airgraph

Dear John,

Just sent off the snaps, they will take a while to come ordinary mail. Helen and Betty are on holiday this week so No. 1 is very quiet. The war news is very bright so here's hoping.

I am planting white lily bulbs this week so I am wondering if you will see them bloom. I hope so. Nan and Roxie were in today. Roxie is a bit shaky after her operation on her tonsils. The weather has been wet here but we should have some good days yet. Remember the September races? Your pop was always going to make a fortune, aye sliding hame* skint.* He is taking a week's holidays, we will be having a day here and there. It will be a change from the normal baking.

Jean is home now, she will be helping me and Betty will get out to business. You will see a big change in the snaps. Twa* smarters, believe me.

Love from mother x x

It would appear my grandfather enjoyed spending his leisure time either drinking a few beers in a pub or betting on the horses. His most popular hostelries were in the Sandgate not far from his work.

Ayr Town Hall on the Sandgate.

12th September 1944

Airgraph

Dear John,

Received your letter with Syria snaps. They are fine. I like the one in the Garden of Eden best. What places you have seen, but I'm glad you think your home will be best. This is lovely September weather. Pop is talking about going for brambles. We are taking down all our black out on September 17th. Ha. Ha. Good going letting in God's holy light. We are glad the war news is so good. The girls are enjoying your lovely tan. They ain't so pale themselves. You will be getting snaps soon, they are on their way. Plums have all been eaten. We had a splendid crop of them and apples. Saw Tony the other day. he looked like a dish cloot.* Well John keep the kites rolling, I'm sorry, flying and hope to be seeing you soon. Love from all at home.

Mother x x

Passenger steamer on the Nile

1ˢᵗ October 1944

Airmail

Dear John,

This is Sunday night so thought I would give you a few lines. I have been twice at church today. It was communion today. I really like Dr Forgan as a preacher. I heard in a round about way that David has been in hospital. I am hoping he has recovered by now. Dysentery it was. A chap in the bakery told father. He had a letter from his brother who is out beside David and he had mentioned that David was in hospital so that is how we got to know. You have been lucky John and kept well so far. We are into October now and it is quite cold tonight leaves swirling along the road. Give me the good old springtime. Maybe I will be preparing for your return in the spring. Well

I have news for you. Betty is working at MacArthur's. Mrs ???? of Trinity is the boss. She is being trained as a saleswoman. You know, seeing auld hens*, they look marvellous in a hat and getting it sold. She likes it fine. She will get a good training. She got the job right away. He had a lot of girls after it but nane* suited but oor Betty. She is very like you everyone thinks. We gave the snaps into Boots, they thought them fine. I am sending off your pyjamas, (is that the richt* spelling, I don't think it.) I have a bit of soap also so I am getting them off tomorrow.

Pop has a cold and believe me he hates not being fighting fit. One day I told him he should pay us for washing his white coats. And before I went out I told him to sort the cord of a window that would not open. Also a bed light needed sorted. So when I came home from town this poem was written for me, he had got the job done and was away to bed. We were in fits laughing at it, Helen, Betty, Jean and I.

'Oh dear Mrs White, always with the money you are so tight
Never wrong but always right
3 coats you said I had to pay
My but you keep me in mind of auld Johnnie Hay.
You will get fresh air at night and the lamp will light
And my bill will square yours and that will be right.

Is it no guid. Anither* Rabbie Burns. I tell you we get many a laugh at him. Have those snaps not arrived yet? David has got his and says what a laugh he had at Mr & Mrs White. Well John, space is about up. We have the house to ourselves now and having the pleasure of it. Nan, Ronald and Roxie were over on Saturday. They are all well. It is a busy hoose.* Mind the day you let her fall out of bed. Whit a row I gave you. Well John these are memories dear. Love from all here

Mother x

And all my love John. Betty x x x

16th October 1944

Airmail

Dear John,

Mother calling you. Glad you liked the snaps. I expect you see a great difference in the grand children but not so much in your mum and dad. We have a few more grey hairs. We are now into the cold weather and boy I like beside the fire. I was at the church yesterday. We had a young minister from Largs and everybody thought he was so clever. This is Monday and a holiday here so we went to the pictures. Ginger Rodgers in 'The Dark Lady', Betty and Helen are saying I'm daft.* It was 'Lady in the Dark.' Nan was away to Edinburgh for the weekend with Jenny Spiers. We were minding Ronald and Roxie. It would be a change for her to get away without the kids. They were staying at a hotel. I'll be getting all the gen about it when I see Nan. Mrs Cowan has been in bed for 6 weeks. Her heart is not in the best condition.

Well John, pop butts in but here goes,
Nellie sits upon the chair
Watching the girls doing their hair
All of a sudden she lets out a yell
Is this no just like your maw*, Nell.
I want you to put a line or two down
Looking over at me with a frown
This I am doing just for her to please
Mither* to sleep with her mind at ease.

She is so like Johnny Hay.
Get out those lights as I have the bills to pay.
She took me Strathaven for a trip
and took me in for fish and chips.
Being no fish we got peas instead.

What a racket there was in bed.

This is just like you maw*, trying out that wee ????.

'Fir aw the arts the wind can blaw '

Time marches on John. Wishing you were home. Also David and Bill so as Nellie and I could share in a wee gill. In the meantime John, the best of luck. Letters will follow soon, faither.

Hello John, Helen here. You're getting a wee bit from everybody tonight. What do you think of our poet? Rabbie Burns hasn't a look in. Quite a jack of all trades. It was the holiday here today and we were all at the pictures. Am getting ready to start work tomorrow, washing of hair, stockings etc. Mother is hounding us on and telling us we won't be in bed till midnight. Hope you are still keeping well John and you got the parcel alright. The girls in Boots are very helpful when we say we are sending a parcel. Will close John but will write soon. It won't be so very long now so keep that chin up.

Lots of love H.

Nice to know my grandfather wrote poetry but none has survived apart from what I have discovered in these letters. He also enjoyed dressing up to entertain guests at home and telling humorous stories.

5th November 1944

Airmail

Dear John,

Here we are again with a few lines. This has been a mild day here with rain and wind. I just took a long lie and had breakfast and dinner in bed, no bad having three daughters to attend to me. The dinner was a treat, they can all cook and bake, that will stand them in good stead in life. The home now is warm. There is a nice fire in the room and Betty is playing the Blue Danube. Pop is having his tea in bed and listening to her, so John we are very happy and comfortable. If the scullery door would open and admit you and David the picture would be complete. Well here's hoping.

Was at the pictures on Saturday with pop. 'Going My Way'. We were at the Gaiety on Friday night. The comic was great and we got a good laugh.

Betty is getting on very well at McArthur's. Helen was at a party on Saturday, a chum's 24th birthday. It was Mrs Cowan that was ill, not him. Ronald has got a rabbit now and a very nice hutch for it. Roxie and him are crazy about it. One night I was up the pair of them were out with matches to let me see it. We have not got Vicky now. It was not well after the last pups so it had to go to the vets. We were upset at the time but have got over it. Betty did love it. I am not a great one for dogs so we have decided to have no more. Nan used to ask Roxie what granny says, 'weans* and dugs'.* Vicky would be flying around the garden, maybe they would be crying.

We are nearing another Christmas and the war goes on. It's a terrible drag on people. Nan has no word from Bill yet. This is Monday and your letter for Helen has come in. I have opened it and those lucky married guys on their way home. You were having two days off and were wise to take a good rest, can't always be on the run. I hate the wet days we are having, no chance of getting down to the bus station and away for a run. However I must get a weekend at Strathaven to see auld Jenny. I'll cut out the peas and chips, it will be safer.

I was away up at Coylton last week. Went up to the cottage where my mother was reared. Enjoyed the outing and got some wallflower plants for my garden. Nan has arrived in now, the tongues are wagging talking about Xmas. Well John news is scarce so I trust this finds you well. David seems to have quite recovered from his bout. Sorry pop is in bed sleeping at the moment so he can't write any poetry.

Xxx from Roxie to my dear Uncle John. This was Roxie writing, me holding her hand. Well I'll be writing soon.

Dear John, Betty calling. Just arrived in from work and what a night it is. This is the night I go to music so after I get my tea I will get down to practising. Well John I will close now. See and look after yourself. God bless you.

All my love Betty xxx

John at the tented camp in Heliopolis where he spent 4 years.

17th November 1944

Airmail

Dear John,

A line or two before the week ends. Tomorrow, 18th is Willie's birthday so I am sending him a card. Wee David was on the 30th and pop on the 9th. It was quite a busy month. Got your last letter dated 5th November. We get them quite quick now. Aye I'll be gey glad when you arrive back at Ayr Station. Won't be so very long now. You have 4 years behind you now, one can hardly believe it. This is Friday. Pop is off to bed for 2 hours. We are going to the Gaiety. It is Dave Willis so hope it's good. Was at the Odeon last night with aunt Aggie. 'A wing and a prayer' with Don Ameche. Very good it was. What clever chaps those flyiers are. Still I take off my hat for the ground staff who keep them in the sky. I don't ken how to spell fleers so skip it. Ha. Ha. We had our tea at the Market Inn, it was lovely. We fair enjoyed it, just a bit of a change. The weeks seem to fly past. Had Roxie over to sleep as the sweep was going to Nan in the morning. She is up to high doh about Santa, all talk, singing, dressing a doll chatting away to her grandpa. Bill is missing a lot, you ought to see her scrubbing handkerchiefs on a wee wash board., sleeves up. Nan over the back, runs in the blood *Both w*orkers.

This morning was a great storm. I was up making myself a cup of tea then back to bed. I rolled myself up in the bed clothes and listened to it. Pop managed down to the bakery before it started. Willie was off work this week. He had given his back a bit of a jerk so Brand gave him a week. I wish he could get out of those pits. Billy is a great big boy. I can hardly carry him. Jean has plenty to do however she can get a ?? on. Willie is still busy with the brides' cakes, makes a guid* sideline I tell him.

Had a letter from Davd this morning. He is well and the weather a lot cooler. He does not know how you and him are going to stand the winter. I'll buy you both a fur limed overcoat. Well John space is about up so I'll say cheerio and get myself dolled up for the Gaiety. See and keep well and it won't be long before you are sitting beside me. Love from all at No. 1. The wee pink flowers are all out at the front. They look so nice and a great bloom of them. Fondest love from mother x

As well as working in the coal mine Willie had developed skills in bakery and to make some extra money was creating wedding cakes.

The sweep would have been going to clean Nan's chimneys. I remember my own mother getting this done and the preparations made to prevent the house getting covered in soot.

Dave Willis was a well known Scottish comedian of the time. One of his best-known songs was "In my wee gas mask" about an Air Raid Warden.

25th November 1944

Airgraph

Dear John,

Got your last letter. Quite excited about the news that you might be home soon. I would hate the part that you would be banged off somewhere else. We will have patience and see. All well at home. Jean is starting at Hourston's on Monday. Your ma will be on her own again. I'll manage ok. This wee house is easy run, no stairs to climb. The top storey is waiting the return of my airman. Hope the parcels you mention arrive at their destination ok. Kids are now talking a lot about Santa. Nice weather just now. I hear auld Jenny is not very well so I am going a run on Sunday to see her. Betty is in for lunch and when I look at her I see you. You sure are of the Gibson stock. Swine kill has not a look in *(This makes no sense but is what it certainly looks like)*

Love and kind thoughts from mother x x

Hourston's, where Jean started working, was a large. store in the town's High St. It began trading around 1919 selling a wide range of goods. It finally closed in 2019. Thus far Jean has been in the army, worked in a munition's factory, served sweets at a confectioner's in the Alloway area of the town and worked at the baker's Gilchrist.

Ayr High St. today.

30th November 1944

Airgraph

Dear John,

Hello there. Nan has got her parcel ok. All delighted. I was up last night with Mrs Stewart. Roxie was nursing her bunny. Good for Mr Edne??. Be sure and send me a copy every month.

I hear Billy Gilchrist's wife is getting married again. Her grief was short lived. This was David's birthday today. I bought him a horse and cart. He has blue eyes, it is the new comer who has brown. He takes after Jean's side. I am having Mrs Kerr for a fortnight at new year so I won't be so lonely. Her and I get on well and she needs a break. Don't eat much before that Xmas dinner John. All well. Jean is in Hourston's now so here's wishing you all the best and lots of love.

Mother

The newcomer being the latest addition to Willie's family, Billy.

13th December 1944

Airmail

Dear John,

I have started to write you a few lines but this pen ain't too good so excuse the scrawl. Got your last letter and glad you got the snaps and the money. Buying gifts for them all would take some cash, good thing Christmas comes but once a year. I just can't be bothered thinking what to get them all. I'll make it money and they can do what they like.

Was over at Willie's today. He is up to his eyes baking cakes, what a lot of orders he has got. I can see you learning the bakery when you come back and getting into business with Willie. Dr Brand has given him a certificate to say he is *(the next word is long, begins with 'temp' and can't completely work it out)* gosh that's a big yin and I'll bet it's wrang*, unfit for work in the pits, you know what I mean. Too fine a boy to be hacking coal. He is an artist to trade and the pit life just not suit him so Brand says. Well that is the first step. He has still to go before another doctor for the pit so I do hope that he is lucky. He was just verging on a breakdown but has been 5 weeks off his work, but the cake making helps him make a wage and he is feeling a bit better. If the next doctor signs him off he will look for work at the bakery, likely land back at Gilchrist's. Pop will apply for a baker to the Labour Exchange. We will let you know. I was telling him to stay up baking all night and smoking and sally out to the second doctor with *cry blabs?* under his een*. That wid dae the trick, what say you. I sincerely hope he gets out then, don't you.

Aye the next 9 months will surely roll in for you. You'll be getting excited when the time draws near. Mrs Halbert got your letter. She is going to write you. Jean and her are both well. Betty goes in every Sunday afternoon for her tea and keeps them company. We have no gossiping neighbours up here that is one thing I like the peace of it. The sun was out today, made me think of spring. Aye and you told me lies about the price of the bike. Fine ye kent* it wid no gae doon wi me if it wis too dear. Must be a bit of Auld Johnny Hay in me always looking for bargains. Got badly stung with the husband I chose, he was certainly not a good bargain. Ha Ha.

Well John it's suppertime. Need to see whit I can scare up for auld Davie. If he says anything I'll chin him with it. The girls are all at the pictures so yours truly will need to close. I am glad you are well , see and be looking after yourself. We will be sending you a bit of dough when pop gets his bonus, after New Year it is. We will be round him like a swarm of bees. The children have all got their toys and pleased they are with them. So here's sending you all my love and will be writing you soon again.

Mother x x

From family stories it is apparent that his children thought 'pop' wasted much of his money on gambling and in pubs so the comment on him not being a good 'bargain' may mean more than just a joke. I believe Johnny Hay, mentioned in several letters, was a real person and a bit of a character around town.

The comment about '9 months' seems to indicate that my father would have served his time in the RAF, or at least be sent back to Britain even though no one knew at this point when the war would end.

Some of John's friends imitating Hitler, Mussolini, Sheik of Arabia and Stalin.

21st December 1944

Airmail

Dear John,

Another few lines from home. Tomorrow 22nd your wee sister Betty will be 16. Getting on and quite the young lady. And what a sunny nature, always bright and gay. She is very well liked at McArthur's. She wears a navy-blue dress with a white collar, looks the essence of smartness. They are very busy now for Christmas. I hear all about the sales she makes. It is a busy house in the mornings getting three hustled out for 9 o'clock. Yours truly lies till the door closes.

The kids are up to high doh about Xmas. Miss Roxie talks all the time about Santa. Nan left her one day with me. When pop came in she was up on a chair doing her hair and asking what he would like from Santa. She is a great girl. When Nan and I are talking we have to spell things as she is listening to every word. No word through from Bill yet. I often wonder how he is getting along. It is a year since Nan had the postcard. I have not received one of your Toc H papers yet. The editor should not forget requests.

Pop is telling me that old McGraw is being asked to quit also Mr Miller so it is great what can happen. Mr Gilchrist would like them out of the place. He has been ill and away in Surrey so Dr. John Gilchrist and a lawyer were sent to see to the matter so I will let you know what happens. Dr John thought that pop's services to the firm should be recognised. I hope it won't take the form of a massive wreath at the heels of the hunt. 35 years he has been with them and worked more than hard so we'll see. I see that May Wilson, Billy's wife is engaged again. Did not mourn long for Billy.

The weather is quite mild at present. I don't think that we will have a white Xmas. There is a great scarcity of whiskey this year, a lot of people will have no Ne'erday bottle, well the big heid* will be missing in the morning so it will be worth not having it. My brother William has got me a bottle so I will be drinking your health on Hogmanay. The girls were asking me what I would like for my Christmas. I should have said a dictionary as some of the words beat me.

Well John space is up. I go out with Aggie on a Thursday night. Tea at the Market Inn and then the pictures so I'll need to get dressed. I'll post this on the way. Hope you are well John and here I am sending you all my love and hope you will be at home by another Christmas and I can make your dinner.

Best wishes for a happy Christmas.

Mother x x

Gilchrist's was the bakery my grandfather worked at for many years. It was known as 'The Land of Burns' bakery and was situated in Boswell Park in Ayr. As well as the bakery there was a popular restaurant and was used for wedding receptions. Like so many things the business and buildings no longer exist. It was eventually taken over by national giant Rank Hovis McDougall.

Toc H mentioned in the letter was a religious organisation founded in 1915 during the Great War. They were set up to provide Christian fellowship and social service. I am not sure how this would involve my father although it looks as if he was a member.

A photograph sent home to his mother

27th December 1944

Airmail

Dear John,

A few lines from me before the old year flies. What a week last one was. Xmas cards galore and quite a few presents. The grand children were greatly excited by it all. I think I can remember buying you a big rocking horse and you were scared stiff to sit on it. Well those days are over for me now. The children got your sweets okay. Their jaws went well I can tell you. David's girl sent them all a minding also.

Nothing new at home to report. I am more a lady now with Betty helping me. Nice to be in bed, Elizabeth up, the fire put on and lovely tea and toast made for me. Then I relax, listen to the wireless and read my mail. Believe me it's fine and I have the brains to know that and enjoy it. She is getting on fine at piano and plays me nice waltzes. Nice to listen to.

I wonder when I'll see you coming in the door and what you will be like. I went away on a good long walk on Sunday and I enjoyed it. I think rolling about the fire is nae use. Martin Meldrum lost his wife last week. She died very suddenly. Her youngest son was killed in the war, that upset her greatly. Best not to build castles in the air these days.

Mrs McMillan is still on the other side of me, her son is away also, so she has to live alone, not so very nice for her. Kenneth Caddell is still at the aerodrome at Prestwick and just as quiet. Nance works at County Buildings. Will and Ailsa both out at work. She teaches at Beith school. I wonder if the weans* there still think the feminine of duke is duck. Whit an alert lassie yer mither must have been. Boots still in the same place, some dithery looking gals in it.

Well John I've nae main news. Ronald is getting a fine big boy. Goes most of Nan's messages. He is a great lad, comes over a lot. Kids me on to make pancakes and toast and whit a boy fur ????? loves it. Miss Roxie is a wee smarter. Bill must have some sad thoughts thinking of them. The only ray of hope is that they have a very wise and capable mother. Cheerio John and a very happy new year.

Mother x x

30th December 1944

Airmail

Dear John,

Here I am again with the last of this year, 1944. The excitement is getting keen for Hogmanay, for a drap* of whisky. My brother William got me some so I am ok. I'll drink your health and be thinking of you as we enter another year. Mrs Kerr is here so it's nice company. I have been gathering wood at the river Ayr gates. A lot of the trees have died and so they were sawing them at the roots and when they fell they splintered a lot. I got on the crack with the workmen, boiled their tea and made them pancakes and what a stock of wood I have so I will have a log fire.

(Pop adds a few lines)

Dear John

I wish you all the very best for 1945. May you come home soon. Your mother and I are going to have a nice time together while I am here John. She is a dear good soul. We will think of you tonight at 12pm and drink your health and pray for your safety until you return to us again. God bless you and best wishes from Mr and Mrs Kerr and every good wish.

I am writing this at the room window and it is a beautiful spring like day. Nan and the two R's were over for dinner *(Ronald and Roxie)*. Roast fowl, mashed potatoes green peas then steamed apple sponge. It was voted a first class dinner. Mrs Kerr and Nan are away up the river Ayr for a walk. I said I would write to you and David. Nan has had a postcard from Bill and he sends us all best wishes. He had received some snaps also so we are all quite pleased. Once the new year is over the months will fly past for you John.

(And later on my grandfather added some more lines) John, pop calling. Nellie says she has got to go for the fire. What an inspiration for me to recall the old song that means a ???. Well John here it is...

'The log was burning brightly

I was alright that would banish all sin

Fir the bells were ringing the old year out and the new year in.

I am just about to make a toast for the new year John and I am including you and David in it. I take the glass into my hand and drink to all that's here.

It's hard to say where we all will be before another year.

Maybe dead, some may wed, some may be lying low.

Some may be on a foreign shore

others not knowing where to go.

So while going up the hill of prosperity may you have health and happiness and a happy new year.

From your loving father.

Christmas dinner in Egypt. My father's table is on right near the back.

1945

10th January 1945

Airgraph

Dear John,

Received your circle Toc Hs. Will be reading them all then give them to Mr Miller. I notice one says the lights are burning in the old homestead. They sure will be as long as your ma is around. I have sent off a little cash for your leave. Cook's will be asking you to call soon. You'll be stepping to your chin that day. *(An expression I am unsure of).*

Mrs Kerr is still here. We are having some nice times together. Billy Honeyman's mother was buried last week. I saw Billy at the funeral. Mind the good fun he and David had at the plays. The weather is nice at present. I am casting a furtive eye at the garden and planning a few jobs to be done as soon as the weather will allow. One fine day I will have to crack the whip and they will all have to jump to it. Will be writing you a letter soon.

Love from mother x x

Nellie outside her beloved home.

20ᵗʰ January 1945

Airmail

Dear John,

Got a letter from you this morning. So here are a few lines in return. The headlines of today's news is that Willie has got his release from the pit. Is that not grand? We are all delighted at home. He is going back to baking. Pop is going to ask for him to be made 2nd hand, able to take the reins when pop's day is up. I am awaiting my beloved coming in. If there is any news I'll add it.

Dr. Forgan was in yesterday. I have given him your letters so the girls have to get them at Bible Class. Then we will give them to Mr. Millar. The minister said he would like to read them. He said he had a letter from you and was very pleased about it. He has only a housekeeper now. His son has been 3 years in Burma. Willie and pop are in now. Willie had to go to the ministry of labour and Girdwood want a man and have first claim on him. He had been to see the manager and he was quite keen to engage him. He was up talking to father. He would like him too and he thinks he would get on very well at Gilchrist's.

This is Sunday now and Willie turned down Girdwood as it was for night work. He had to get a doctor's line before they would allow him to say no, so Brand said do that so he starts at Gilchrist's as I told you carrying on where pop stops. Excuse this hurried note John as I would like to post it just now as I know you will be pleased to know all about Willie. I will write you through the week when I have more time. Nan was in with Roxie just now. They are away to get the girls and all go to the pictures. Sunday is communion so I am going with Aggie. I heard aunt Agnes say she got your airletter. They don't bother writing much now do they?

Love from all. Mother x x

PS The months will fly John. Be of good cheer.

John is on the extreme right of the back row

26th January 1945

Airmail

Dear John,

Got your letter telling me you had been moved to Greece. I am wondering how you like that. They were not long in getting you shifted when they knew you were not doing much. Well I thought you were going on leave and sent on £8 by Cook's so you will let me know if you get it. Will they send it on to you? Anyhow you can see about it at your end. It was sent on the second week of January so you will maybe get leave where you are. We are having a very cold spell at Ayr. You would get my letter telling you that Willie was back to the baking. He is jolly glad to get away from the coal industry. I am glad you are enjoying your food, what wid a no gie to be making your dinner. Will you be getting home this year?

Remember Mr. Munro often called Monkey Munro. He is very ill, won't get better, cancer he has. He is kept doped all the time. What one is called on to suffer. He has swallowed some whiskey in his days. Took your letters into Mr Millar. Dr. Forgan had enjoyed reading them. How did you like the air trip John? I would have been scared stiff. Pop is in for his dinner and telling me Mr Munro is dead. He is another figure we will see no more. News is kind of scarce. Had a photo from Joyce. She is very nice in it. Had a letter from David. He is still pegging away. Kind of dreading the bad weather coming but it is cold enough at present.

Well John space is about up. I will write you very soon and I hope you are happy enough in your new surroundings. Let me know how you are getting on and see about the money I sent. Pop has a cold but otherwise we are all well. Love from everybody over here and keep your chin up, all will be well.

Love from mother x x

At this time my father had been posted from Egypt to mainland Europe and from the letter obviously flew to Greece.

12th February 1945

Airmail

Got your letter dated February 4th so it did not take too long to come. I write to Edinburgh (Books) and told them you have moved to Greece. You will see about getting it anyway. If you write a letter authorising one of your chums to get it or send them your new address I expect they will send it to you.

We were wondering if we could send you a parcel, we will do our best, not so easy these days due to rationing. Potatoes are scarce here I am getting a bag through Helen talking to a farmer or would it be the farmer's son. I wonder. Her boss met with an accident coming from Stranraer. The time of the snow. He came away from his side of the road as there was a huge drift of snow and another car went smack into him. Broke his leg and 2 stitches in his head. Helen goes out to his home in Stair and takes his letters then types them at the office. Good head has Helen and very methodical.

Betty is so clever at baking and cooking. She was making toffee the other night, a whole tin of condensed milk in it. I was telling her very extravagant and I allow you to do it. Aw well it's all gaun* doon* the wan* road. She brought me a bunch of snowdrops today. They are lovely flowers, the heralders of spring. I can't see my white lilies coming up yet. I was telling pop they would be great ones seeing I bought them in his home town Hamilton. We will wait and see, they will need some heat I expect. It is pouring of rain here today. I have been mending and sewing. Just waiting for the girls coming in for tea. Mince and doughballs. Never mind, I'll do nothing but cook for you when you come home. Surely the war will soon be over.

Nan is away to Glasgow to see Margaret Smith. She used to go with her. She is married and lives in Glasgow. Her husband is a detective so I bet Nan is enjoying herself, also Miss Roxie. Margaret has two boys so she will be in love with Roxie. Don't talk about being shy with the girls, they are fair excited about you coming home. All the grand children are to be over the first day and stay overnight. You ought to see Ronald, a picture. The lassies are sending him love letters at the school. I bet you got some too Jake.

All our love, mother x x

27th February 1945

Airmail

Dear John,

Got your letter dated 22nd so that is quick work this being the 27th is it not. No it was Mr Lockhart who met with the accident but he is getting better now. By jove I'll better get in a gey* lot of coal for you boys coming home. We are getting the nice days. The grass has that very fresh green look about it and the snowdrops and crocuses showing. The buds are out on the lilac tree and the birds have started their love songs. I do like the spring.

So you saw old Churchill. We saw him at the pictures taken in Athens and the crowds and I was just wondering if oor* John was among them. I just think he overdoes it with the cigar, aye and his mooth.*

John Smith is now married. He was discharged from the forces and is back in the pub. Yon is an awful miserable woman, his mother. I bet John's wife won't like her. They have rooms at Park Circus. Guess they will have to pay for them there. Peggy and Jessie can't get a lad at all. David was going on leave in Bombay. My you boys have seen the places. I'm very pleased with my own fireside but I'll hear all about the places you have been when you come home. Cheerio for now, mother.

Dear John, Betty calling. Just finished reading a murder book called, 'Lady in distress'. It gave me the creeps. Got a new pair of summer shoes today. Pop bought me them. I sure feel swanky in them. They are open-work and the colours are blue and tan. Feeling rather tired tonight as I've had a very busy day at the shop. (Tuesday, market day.) I sold about £26 worth of goods. Not bad at all. The coupons have certainly put the dampener on some of us extravagant young ladies. Mother says we would have her in the poor house if she fell in with all our wants. But I must say they are a good father and mother to us. What say you John? Was up at my music last night and Miss Ward said I was becoming quite a good player. I felt very pleased with myself as she usually doesn't tell you such things. My new piece is called 'Wandering' by Schubert. Well John I'm afraid that's all I have room for so I'll sign off. See and take care of yourself and only hope it won't be long till your home.

All my love your wee sister Betty xxx

Winston Churchill visited Athens in December 1944 to use his influence in negotiations between the Greek government and the communist-led resistance group, the National Liberation Front. His aim was to create a provisional government and avoid the outbreak of civil war and to keep Greece free of communist control. At the time, Athens had recently been liberated from Axis forces, but it was still beset by tensions between the Liberation Front and British forces and there had been armed clashes.

9th March 1945

Airmail

Dear John,

A few lines as usual. The spring days are here, the sun was quite warm yesterday, so I spent it in the garden working. The painter has done the kitchenette, painted the walls cream. It is nice and bright. Yes you just make out the menu you would like when you arrive home, and I'll do the rest. Mr Millar got your address so he must be going to write to you. I hope you got your money ok. Tell me in the next letter. You will not be able to get any good feeds in that hungry hole, a change from Cairo.

David might come under the leave scheme and be home along with you. Would that not be grand? I do wish this war would finish up, it seems endless. Nothing new John just the same routine every day. Nan and Helen were away at Glasgow seeing what they could get for the spring. I had Roxie over for the day. She was washing the steps and busy as a bee. Good wee girl and smart.

They are shorthanded at the bakery just now, can't get men very easy so that means the rest have more to do. Willie is very glad to be out the pits. The miners are on strike at present. Want bigger pays. I say they should get it as it is a rotten job they have got, dangerous as well. News is kind of scarce John. This is Friday. Pop and thought of going to Strathaven a run on Saturday. I hear that auld Jenny is not grand these days. She is 94 years old and what a busy energetic life she led. She will be nearing the end of the road. We will enjoy the run, just hope the sun is shining. Well John I'll ring off, here is Betty to add a line. Love from mother x.

Just in from work John and boy do I feel tired. Old bitches in trying on hats. 'You know that's not what I wanted. I think my style of face suits a nice big brim. Anything to hide their dials. Ha! Ha! The war is certainly going great guns. Let's hope it keeps up. Well John that's all I've got room for so cheerio just now. Look after yourself.

Love Betty x x x

The details of allowing servicemen and women to leave the armed services involving the criteria and framework for demobilisation were unveiled to the public on 22 September 1944. It was scheduled to be implemented on 18 June 1945. However, this letter seems to indicate that there was some hope Willie would be home sooner rather than later.

15ᵗʰ March 1945

Airmail

Dear John,

Got your letter this week ok. Glad you are well. Pop was so please at the compliment of being young looking nae wunner* he worries aboot* buggar all and has good nerves. He says if he had not, that bakery at the present day would have got him down. Then he gets plenty of rest and not a sound in the garden. Anyway I intend that the sleeping hours shall be reduced as there is a lot of work to be done. You leave it to me. I'll buck up their ideas for them.

Wee David has the measles and bronchitis so that is not good. I think I'll have him over here when he is better for a change. The good fresh air here would do him good.

I was up at the river Ayr with Roxie. We filled two wee bags with the nice earth. It improves the soil in the garden. The crows were making a hell of a row at their nest building. Roxie was fair enjoying it. Cheeks like roses she has. We are all busy getting the place in ship shape. At the end of this month is Glasgow spring holiday weekend. I have some of my regulars returning. Aye I would have liked you home in the good old summertime but I'll have a big stock of coal in, you will be a right warm house plant. A guid fire and a guid meal, you won't be calling the king your cousin.

Went to Strathaven and saw auld Jenny. She was so pleased to see us. She is a good bit frailer. Her daughters were in. I could see they were not making the tea to please her and not make her angry at not being able to do it herself. She has always been so managing herself that it makes her ratty looking at them. Kind of like that myself. Was away at Monument last night with Aggie and Nan for tea, very enjoyable, a refreshment before it. Pair of us sitting with earrings in, very swanky. The Gibsons from Beith ha ha.

Well John I wish the time was at hand for your home coming. I think I have told the whole of Ayr you are coming home. Boy oh boy roll on that day. Maybe the war will soon be over, I'm hoping that. Girls are all at pictures tonight. I'm getting up to date with my mail. Cheerio and keep smiling.

Love from all at home, mother x x

The war in Europe was to end 2 months after this letter on 8th May 1945. I can only imagine the joy and relief it brought to everyone in the town and at Lothian Rd. John and David would be coming home soon.

'The Monument' is a hotel situated in Alloway not far from Rabbie Burns' cottage and a memorial to mark his life. It lies very close to the famous small bridge Tam O'Shanter is said to have crossed when being chased by witches.

Pop with his younger daughters Betty and Helen

31st March 1945

Airmail

Dear John,

Received your letter on 30th March with snaps ok. No John, you have not changed a bit, you are still the same wee boy to your mother. I think you are very like my own dear mother. I see a great resemblance and if you're like your granny in your ways you'll do. As Dr Forgan wrote in your reference 'you will maintain the standard'. Well worth remembering when times are so hard. It will be a year tomorrow (Sunday) that his wife died. He is in the manse himself with a housekeeper. I expect he will miss his wife at every turn. I'll be at the church tomorrow to hear him.

I have the first of the visitors here and it is pouring with rain. They have all gone to the pictures. Need the good weather to please them. Mrs Kerr is coming on Tuesday for a week so we will be going places together. Kenneth is still at the aerodrome and still so quiet. I think he will pep up a bit outside. Ian is still the same gay boy with the ready smile. Betty says he gets so shy when he sees her. Helen was at a dance at Bellisle (a sweet lasssie and so easily dressed.) I hope when her young man comes along he will be a good one. He will need to be to please our Helen.

Betty is buzzing around as usual, my right hand. We have got the garden all in order, it is so nice with the blossom and I spend a lot of time in it myself. Yes we are all excited at the thought of seeing you. We will relax for a month. I was away at the River St. mission to hear auld Agnes singing, John's wife. She is quite a nice singer. Then I heard your play David was in 'Well connected'. Mind David was the father. Billy Gilchrist courting Annie. Poor Billy. A nice chap gone. It was very good but Davie's was better. Not just so crude to their chap.

Well I'm listening to Bing Crosbie on the wireless. He is good. Wee David is a lot better. He was over last Saturday with Willie playing a wee shop. Well John, space is about up. This is students' day. The slogan is

'Any sum chum' instead of the usual 'Any gum chum.' I'll be writing again soon. I will send you the Ayr Aid magazine, there are some laughs in it. Aye auld Johnny Hay. He passed on quite suddenly. He missed his wife's care, sitting with wet clothes on and got a chill. Love from us all to your dear self.

    Mother x x

Agnes Gibson, Nellie's mother and who she thinks John bears a great resemblance to.

22nd April 1945

Airmail

Dear John,

Sorry I missed writing you last week, but here I am again. We are having lovely weather just now and I have been out quite a lot. Was at Beith with Agnes a run in the bus. The countryside is a picture just now. I am just home from church tonight. Willie was there and aunt Caddell. There was a very poor attendance. Dr Forgan did not look very pleased.

I hear Bert Catto is home just now. I have never met him. He had been over at Mr Cowan's shop to see him. Rona Cowan has another son today, she wanted a wee lassie as she has a boy already. A weel there's no sending back the goods, tak whit ye get and be pleased or no. Yesterday 21st April was my birthday, 55. I am, my my, I'm getting old. Had a lot of cards from the grandchildren and friends. Joyce must have notified Brownlees as I had a dozen lovely tulips sent up. Very kind thought, just like the girl. She believes in things being done right. Nothing erratic about her. Betty and Helen are dancing just now, no be this the morn's morning. A cousin, Jimmy Gilchrist has got a year of the jail and fined £2000 for defrauding the income tax people. Fool that he was, might have known it would come to light sooner or later.

Hello John, Helen here. How are you? We've been having a taste of the heat this week and we've been out in it every possible moment. 'Music while you work' is on. Betty and I were trying a jig but there's something wrong somewhere. It aye ends up in a carry on. Betty is good fun. Mother is always telling us to practise for you coming home, what a job you're going to have. We are all looking forward to our holidays. I think it has been a rather trying winter with one thing and another, but the news is great, only 2 miles from the suburbs of Berlin as I write this. It shouldn't last much longer. Our boys and the allies have done a great job – that's including my big brothers. These Japs have still to be beaten but they'll not be so long either when we can concentrate on them alone. We won't know what's wrong when it's over! Well time is slipping past quickly and it won't be long till you're ringing the bell at No. 1 John. Here's to that day. See and take good care of yourself. Lots of love from all.

Helen x x x x

'Music While You Work' was a daytime radio programme of continuous live popular music broadcast in the United Kingdom twice daily on workdays from 23 June 1940 until 29 September 1967 by the BBC.

The programme began in World War II with the idea that playing non-stop popular light music at an even tempo would help factory workers become more productive. It originally consisted of live music being played by light orchestras as well as dance, brass and military bands.

It was aired twice daily on workdays from 23 June 1940 until 29 September 1967 by the BBC.

The war with Japan ended on 15th August 1945 after two atomic bombs were dropped, one on Hiroshima and the other on Nagasaki at the beginning of August.

2nd May 1945

Airmail

A line or two as usual. Observe the date and we are all shivering with the cold. Sleet and hailstones at the end of April. Freak weather before that it was very warm then. This has blighted the rose and fruit trees and done a lot of damage. Well what's cooking big boy?

We were away at Kilmarnock yesterday, Nan, Betty and I. They were looking at frocks. I was wondering what I could get for my stomach. Then I told them to go on their own for half an hour. I disappeared to my haunts on side streets and got myself two posh hats, been bought at MacDonalds of Glasgow and Edinburgh by some lady, well it's a lady that has them now. I was the only person who did business. The frocks they liked were too expensive so they are going to Prestwick another day. There are one or two nice shops there. Anyway we enjoyed the afternoon. Had ice cream then our tea.

Today I am at the fire, been sewing a bit and got a great big dumpling on for tea. Nan is coming in. I have Roxie here. Nan is away at the nursing home seeing Donna's new baby another son. So you can picture us round the table and the dumpling getting big licks. I have the raisins you sent in it so it should be guid. Are you smacking your lips at the thought of it? Willie has arrived in now with wee David, he is your double. He is reading to him and Roxie a Jack and Jill story. You ought to see them. Nan is in now. She is telling me she has got her new dress in wee McCulloch's. it's next to Hugh Forbes. Aye the money was burning a hole in her pocket. I am going to the pictures with pop now. They are showing the German atrocities in the prison camps. Helen and Betty were at it and were in tears at what they saw. My we should be very humble and thankful at being spared such a fate.

Thanks for the box with the nuts and the raisins. They arrived ok. Bert Catto and his wife are invited over to Jenny Spiers, she will be making something for them. Jenny is a lovely cook. Nan has brought home a lot of Hourston's dirty flags. They have been lying since the coronation. They have been washed and starched and Ronald has had two of them away. They are worth something as the flags in the shops are very dear. Well John I've no more news. I have folks from Largs at present and this cold weather does not suit them. I've got all my cleaning and garden done so I mean to be out plenty. Willie McMurdo? Was in today, he was saying you had planted the lilac tree at the front. Did you? Well it is in bloom now and looks lovely. Won't be long till you are coming in the gate. Pop will be playing his favourite record, 'You are as welcome as the flowers in May.

Love Mother x x

The chorus of the song quoted is as follows -

You're as welcome as the flowers in May
And we love you in the same old way
We've been waiting for you day by day

My father's sister, Helen

28th May 1945

Airmail

Dear John,

Mother calling and sending her love. Trust you are well and happy. The weather is lovely at Ayr. The lilac trees are in bloom again. We have not managed any snaps yet. You would have got the news of Gertie's death. Pernicious anaemia was her trouble but pneumonia set in and she was so low in health she could not stand it. She died at Ballochmyle hospital. We all got a shock. Wee Gertie is 8 and a half years and a smart one.

Had a letter from David. He is telling me he is bringing a girl friend with him on his leave. She is a London girl so David has got tripped up at last. See you and never mind the lassies Jake for a long time. There is a lot to be said for a happy bachelor. He is coming home on the 26th June till 3rd July. We are all jogging along as usual waiting for the war to be over. Pop has sole possession of the hut now. He says he would not change it for a castle. He has it painted cream in the inside. We are planning to go to Edinburgh for a week. Writing to find a room in the town.

I have Roxie over for 2 days. Nan is having a wee holiday. She was in the garden all day, never a word. Pop was playing a wee shop with her. I might take a run to Glasgow soon and send you on some money from Cook's if I can find the place. I got the money refunded from the postmaster general so that was fine. Well John my grand daughter is impatient for me to go to town with her so I'll need to sign off. Hoping you are looking after yourself well. Love from all at home. Roxie sends you a kiss and you have to hurry up and come home.

Love from mother x x

It seems surprising that here is no mention of the war being over in Europe, which ended on 8th May.

This letter makes me wonder if the earlier mentions of David's girlfriend was someone else as this indicates that he has just met Joyce, his future wife..

18th June 1945

Airmail

Dear John,

Here I am again, June 17th, with another few lines. This was Sunday and I have been twice at church and at Nan's so before going to bed I thought I had better write you. It was a beautiful morning but turned to rain at night and was quite windy. I am having the wee shed that pop built down, and Paton's men are rebuilding it. Last Monday morning there were 2000 bricks dumped at the door, cement and tools etc. I was wishing I had left the wee wooden thing. I just thought that they would have built the wall in no time and stuck on a roof but builders don't work that way. Pop and Nan had a good laugh at me. I was out speaking to the man and telling him I thought it would be a wee simple job. I said by the look of it, it is to be the vault for the family jewels. Pop says it is Hatton's Castle. Anyway it will be right and let in no rain. It is for bikes, deck chairs etc. Pop says watch it doesn't end up with a bed in it. They only used some of the bricks but they left a big lot as it is the one haulage, and what is left goes back to the yard.

The folks are here and it is a bit of company. I'm not so keen on the letting now. I like the house to myself, must be getting old. Well the time is rolling on for you. You might get away a bit earlier than you think. A plane crashed beyond Stranraer last week, did not clear the hills. 17 American airmen were killed. Sad for their folks to get that news. Monday is a holiday here. The girls are going a picnic. Let's hope the weather will be good. Willie is up to high doh about a shop that is to let in George Street. It was a home bakery, the chap gave it up for health reasons. Willie thinks he should take it. Of course he would need to see if he could get the license and allocation of materials so don't be surprised if you hear of it. Pop did not back the winner of the Derby, neither did I. Had 4/- on. I've no time for gambling. John Gibson marked the first four horses and won 13/10, no bad. Everything is short here. John don't worry about that. Sultanas and almonds I like but get yourself home that is all that matters. The new potatoes are in now, boy they are grand, I have some planted in the garden, late ones. I'll give you the job of lifting the first ones.

Love from everybody at home. Mother x x

The derby was actually held at Newmarket during the war years. The winner of the 1945 race was called 'Dante'.

2nd July 1945

Airmail

Into July now, the time is flying. I missed writing to you last week as I was so busy. Pop and I are going off tomorrow, Sunday for a holiday. He is taking a fortnight this year. We are going to Stonehouse a week then going to Annan to see his brother. They are both country places so it should do us good.

This is the voting week too, might need to run home for an afternoon to get that done. I know you want Labour, we will see. I will ask if they would like to come to Stonehouse and take us by car to the poll.

Helen is away to Edinburgh for a week with her chum, very nice girl she is. Her father is headman at Cameron's. We have had a heck of a time of rain and thunder & lightning also. I bet the sun will be blazing when pop and I set out. Nice to have a holiday. I leave number 1 in very capable hands. Nan is coming over and it will be a change for her at Lothian Rd. and R and R *(Roxy and Ronald)* like the garden. I'll be leaving a few instructions. I have had a coal house built and a bit added at end of house wall and cement roof on it will dry proof now. You will see all these things when you come home and give me your verdict on them.

Willie is on tenterhooks to see if he has been lucky in getting the permits for the shop. It is in George St. opposite Limond's Wynd. Maybe you remember it. He thinks he could get on fine. Certainly be an uphill fight at first. The bride cake business is often good paying, gifted with clever hands or Wullie. Pop says he will give him a good hand at nights. Be a bit of interest for him. It will be a laugh if Willie can give him a job. Gilchrist's is not sold yet. Price is very high. City bakeries have been looking at it.

Was away at a concert in Academy Hall. Nessie Gibson was in a play, 'Elizabeth refuses' it was splendid. I fairly enjoyed it. Betty was there. She was in fits with the boy who played the clergyman. Nessie is quite the young lady now. Billy has seen a bit of the world like yourself. David was saying he had been going up the hills for a rest but he had to stand down to let some boys who were sick go, so he was one of the unlucky ones. However he will get later on and be more needing it. I wish you were back home and among us. I have to get my case packed. I won't be trailing much away. Your faither and me never went in for much grandeur now did we. Twa simple souls.

Hello John, Betty calling. Well as mother told you she and father are going on holiday. It will do them both good. You ought to see the list of instructions I've been left. Remember laundry, get some plants, don't waste gas and soap powder needlessly. I ken ye. saying tae yersel 'I'll just get another packet in the morn'. Ha! Ha! Here's hoping they get good weather. Cheerio just now. Lots of love, Betty xxx

The final result of the General election showed Labour to have won a landslide victory making a net gain of 239 seats, winning 47.7% of the popular vote and achieving a majority of 145 seats. The new prime minister was Clement Atlee who took over from Winston Churchill. This election marked the first time that the Labour Party had won an outright majority in Parliament, and allowed Attlee to begin implementing the party's post-war reforms for the country. Labour won the South Ayrshire Constituency in which Nellie lived.

The fact that John wanted Labour to win is news to me as I always had him down as a Conservative in my youth although he never actually came out and said it.

12th July 1945

Airmail

Dear John,

A few lines as usual, July 12th. Was on holiday last week so did not get writing you. Pop was with me and we were back to his old haunts, Stonehouse and Strathaven. The weather was ideal so you can guess pop was looking well. I think farmer White would suit better than baker. He started work today preparing for the Glasgow Fair which starts on Saturday so you can guess how busy Ayr is going to be. They won't be able to bake enough.

I hear Willie has got the tenancy of the shop so he waits to see if he can get the permits for sugar, fats etc. He will know by the end of the month. I hope he gets on well, he will have to work very hard to make it pay. However never venture never win. Pop can give him a good hand once he gets started. It is in George St.. You will be getting all the gen on it when you are home.

We have a rain barrel at side of the hut and I was lowering 2 depth charges into it today, 2 bottles of beer, string round their neck. On Sunday I'll ask pop to take a lucky dip. Won't he be pleased? It will be lovely and cool as the weather is very warm at present. Just one of my brain waves but I bet it meets with his approval.

The girls are at the shore bathing this afternoon so I have the garden to myself and am I enjoying it? Helen is on her second week's holiday. She is looking the better of them. Elizabeth is ok, being the boss at Lothian Rd. suits her. Pop has a snap taken with a sun helmet on. I better not send any snaps. You will be seeing the models in person. We will send them to David, he will get a laugh. I got the hat for 4/-. It had been bought in Oxford St. in London so we will have 4/- laughs. Father had it on and shorts and posing about the garden with it on. Lord Haw Haw. We were in fits and the people in the house. I should make a charge for entertaining them.

Was up at Nan's in a very posh car belonging to Mr Gibson of Hamilton. His manager has the loan of it while he does a year in jail for defrauding the government. A laugh is it not. He was up seeing father (the manager) so gave us a run up to Nan's. A Buick it was, upholstered in pale grey, the essence of comfort. I would be grateful for an auld tin lizzie if it could run me about.

Well John time is drawing on for your leave. You won't be able to relax until you are on the boat. Then you will be singing 'Rolling home tae bonnie Scotland'. Well we are well and that is a lot to be thankful for. Let me know when you can when you are leaving. I am wondering how long the boat will take to bring you over. Well cheerio. See to watch nothing happens to prevent you getting away.

Love from everybody. Mother x

Lord Haw-Haw was a nickname applied to William Joyce and several other people who broadcast Nazi propaganda to the United Kingdom from Germany during the Second World War. The broadcasts opened with "Germany calling, Germany calling," spoken in an affected upper-class English accent.

Joyce was hung for treason in 1946, the last person to be hung for that crime in Britain.

Pop possibly wearing the hat Nellie bought for him.

19th July 1945

Airmail

Dear John,

Another few lines before you leave. This is Glasgow Fair and Ayr is packed. I am as usual busy. Will be glad when they all get away and I get the house to myself. We are all getting our lugs* back for you coming. Time is rolling on and it won't be long till you are coming down Ashgrove St. wonder what you will see different in Ayr.

Weather has been real broken this week and the Glasgow folk don't like rain. They are quite pleased if the sun shines. Had the Stonehouse folk through for a few days. They like Ayr very well.

Pop was saying there were half a dozen gentlemen through the bakery yesterday. It seemed to upset him a bit. He would rather know that the boss was well and able to carry it on. Seems to be a family squabble but time will tell. Jimmy's health has cracked up. Of course he was a man that lived on his nerves.. I'm a bit that way myself and it wears you out if you let it master you. Pop is best, come night, come day, easy going. This is the first time I have seen him kind of nervy, thinking of the bakery changing hands. I tell him away and don't be daft, with your credentials you can hold your heid high.

Willie won't know about the shop till the end of July. He is definitely to get it, if he can get the materials from the food office. Had a letter from David, it was full of plans for his wedding, get married when he is demobbed then get a job and live at Ayr. She is a nice girl so all should be well. Don't you be in a hurry Jake, married life brings worries too. Better be a gay bachelor for a time and enjoy freedom. Mrs Bolton would be very pleased with the flowers but very sad too I should think. Funny you were able to get all that done and your brother going to marry her sister. They seem to be a very nice family.

Time marches on when I think of you all at Craigie Avenue playing about. I thought it was a great guddle* and maybe it was my best days. Well John news is scarce so I'll close and trust all is well with you and here's to seeing you very soon. Love from everybody back home and a lot from me.

Mother x x

John with his sister Betty, on the left, and Helen.

Other Letters

The following letter was sent to my grandmother by her son David. It was sent on November 21st 1945.

Dear Mother and all,

This is just a few lines this evening to say I am leaving here for Bombay in the morning at 9.30. I've been round saying 'cheerio' to some of my mates and have just been writing to Joyce , so it gets a wee bit late now and I can't make this a long letter.

Was very pleased to get a last letter from you today dated the 12th and it was fine to read all about Jean's wedding. I'm glad everything went off ok and I'm pleased they got the wine Joyce sent from us both. I'll be home by Xmas I think so I'll see Jean and her husband before they leave. I'm not sure what place I'll arrive at yet but I hear we get demobbed at a place near Birmingham. And they say it takes 4 or 5 days there to get the civvy clothes etc, Heavens I'll be sending a wire saying I've arrived safely. I would like to have Joyce with me when I come home, so don't be surprised to see us both at the door.

I'll be writing again when I arrive at Bombay of course, and maybe I can tell you then when my boat is due to arrive in Blighty. I think we might be in Bombay for a few days but it will all depend if there is a boat waiting.

I was pleased to get the few lines from John and I am glad he got time off to be at the wedding. Joyce was telling me he was at a place called Linton-on-Ouse but I see he doesn't like the 'grub' too much. A well it won't be long before we are all in civvy street again. Say hello to him for me when you write and tell him I'm hoping to see him at the New year.

Well that's all my news for now, so I'll say 'cheerio' from here but will be writing as soon as I reach Bombay. I was telling Joyce I'll no sleep in the morn.

I am unsure where in India David was serving but it was in some capacity with the RAF with 214 Squadron I am presuming that the war has ended and that the letter was sent in 1945.

Nellie's daughter Jean married her husband O.B. Acker in 1945 and was almost immediately planning to go to the States.

Jean on her wedding day. Helen is the bridesmaid.

The following letter was written to my father at Lothian Rd. by one of his wartime chums called Jack. I believe his second name was Parkinson. Obviously my father had returned home after his war was over.

21st October 1945

Dear Jock,

How's the leave going down Jock? I am on a crafty 48 hour at the moment. I was posted from ??? on Thursday to 71 base in Waddington near Lincoln. I arrived there Friday night after having a day at home to find there was no such unit as 71 Base there. I had to report to the (dis) orderly room at 8.30 the next morning and they had found out that 71 base was at Lyndhome near Doncaster. They got Lyndhome on the phone and asked if they were expecting me and they said they had my posting from records and it had said I was posted for duty at 71 base at Scunthorpe, they had just sent a signal to records asking them what this duty at Scunthorpe was as there are no RAF places in Scunthorpe, certainly none of theirs anyway and it's about 30 miles away. They've told me to hold on at Waddington until they get some 'gen' back from records. The officer in the orderly room at Waddington gave me a 48 hour pass to pacify me as I was carrying on about 'typical RAF etc'. So here I am Jock, but what a game eh!! It was the same when we left Regent's Park. The whole PDC in a convoy with the officers leading in a car. They'd been once to look at the joint , they had road maps and this place was only 19 miles. It took us 4 hours. They got lost and we near travelled around the whole country. What a camp as well! It was one of those dromes, scattered all over the countryside. Fancy having a place like that for a PDC.

Well if you drop me a line send it here as you see I'm not static yet and anyway I shall be home quite a lot if I go to Lyndholme which I think is pretty certain. Remember me to all at 1 Lothian Rd, especially Helen. I'll bet it shook you when you saw your sisters after 4 years didn't it? Is your sister Nan's husband safe? I hope he is.

I'll say cheerio for now Jock, I hope you are having a good leave and don't forget to drop a line soon.

Your old pal

Jack.

PS I had a letter from Chick. He landed home the day you arrived at Regent's Park.

I wonder if Jack had visited Lothian Rd. at some point and taken a shine to Helen. Regent's Park was the place where volunteers to join the

RAF as ground crew went to be trained. The abbreviation P.D.C. means Personnel Despatch Centre and I presume that this is where my father and Jack went before being posted overseas.

It is also apparent from this letter Nan's husband Bill had not returned home or if in fact anyone knew if he was safe.

The Family after the War

I am uncertain as to when my father got home from his war, but I am sure his homecoming would have been a very warm and welcoming one. Nellie's dream of him turning up at the door would at some point have come true.

Unfortunately, Nellie died in 1949, only 4 years later, and never met John's own children or other grand children born to other members of the family.

Although I never knew her, I have learned a lot abut her through her letters, a caring woman with a good sense of humour devoted to her family. But also a woman who seemed to understand the importance of money.

She obviously went out her way to help people and was an astute businesswoman with her bed and breakfast business. She also enjoyed her home and garden where I feel she felt safest but was not afraid to get out and enjoy herself when possible, despite the war and the difficulties it brought.

Pop White remarried, possibly in the early sixties. His relationship with his children after Nellie's death was strained and I only met him twice that I can remember.

The letters may have shown that he was a man who could act the fool and make everyone laugh but through snippets from other family members I suspect that the children felt he had made life difficult at times for Nellie. Perhaps there are some clues here and there in the letters. He died in 1971.

Pop with his second wife.

On returning from the war John returned to Boots for a short time before qualifying as a pharmacist after studying in Glasgow. He went into partnership with a friend, and they ran a Pharmacy in a small Ayrshire village called Tarbolton which was named 'Divine and Gibson' possibly after the maiden names of the two partners' mothers. After a few years he bought his partner out and ran the business for many years retiring due to ill health in the 1970s.

He did remain a 'gay' bachelor for 5 years after the war until he met my mother Kathleen at a dance at Ayr Pavilion and they married in 1950. I came along in December 1951 and my sister in November 1955.

John's wedding day.

He died at home in 1982 in Ayr after suffering many years from Multiple Sclerosis.

Willie and Jean had another child after the war who was named Charles. The family moved to Manchester where Willie ran a bakery business. David, mentioned in the letters became a theatrical agent, Alice married and had as son but got divorced. Billy, born during the war was a house painter. Charles worked for the famous footballer George Best for a few years chauffeuring him around Manchester and running one of his boutiques. Willie died in 2000.

David did marry Joyce as can be seen below. Roxie on the left was a flower girl at the wedding. They had two children. David became a hairdresser and for many years the family lived in Bromley, Kent.

Wedding day. Roxie is the flower girl on the left.

After leaving Scotland Jean and O.B. lived in Dallas, Texas and they had three sons and a daughter. Jean died of a heart attack in Dallas in 1979.

Jean in the USA

Nan's husband Bill did return from his ordeal as a POW and early in the fifties they emigrated to Australia with Roxie and Ronald.

Unfortunately, the marriage did not last, and they were divorced in 1954. Ronald returned to Scotland as he missed the girlfriend he had left behind and they married shortly after. Roxie remained in Australia with her mother where she got married and went on to have 3 sons.

Roxy as a young woman

After the war Helen met and married Hugh and the couple had two children. For a while they lived in Australia but returned home to

Great Britain. The family moved around to many parts of the UK due to Hugh's work but eventually moved back to Ayr where she worked as a secretary for Her Majesty's Inspectorate of schools.

She was the last member of the family to die, passing away in 2022 at the age of 96.

Helen with her sister Nan

Helen & Hugh with their first child.

Helen in 2017

Betty born in 1928 also travelled to Australia and met Peter Graber, a Swiss. They had one child who was born in Australia. At some point the family returned to Britain and as Peter was a baker specialising in cakes, they ran a tearoom and bakery in Bexhill on Sea.

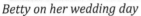

Betty on her wedding day   *With her brother David.*

Despite the family spreading far and wide after the war they kept in close contact with each other through letters and telephone and I fondly remember the visits of my uncles Willie and David with their families back to their hometown on several summers. They would always take back with them to England some Scottish bread and David always added a Scotch pie or two.

But times change and now I only have contact with Helen and Hugh's children. Even the advent of digital correspondence has not allowed Nellie's grandchildren to keep in touch, something which I think would make her sad.

A few extra photographs of myself as a young child with my father John and other family members.

Sitting on John's first car

Story for bedtime

John with myself and his brother David and his son

Holding Helen's hand and with her husband and daughter

Myself and Roxie circa 1953

Visiting my Aunt Nan and Roxi

Index of Scottish words found in the letters

Aboot - about

Aff – off

Anither – another

Auld – old

Auld hens - old women

Aw – all

Awa - away

Awfie - awfully

Bairns - children

Blawing – blowing or showing off

Blaw - blow

Blawn – blown

Braw – fine, handsome

Breeks - trousers

Broo – brow

Cloot - cloth

Dae ye ken - Do you know

Daft – silly

Doon - down

Drap - drop

Drouthy – thirsty

Dugs – dogs

Dunner heid – stupid person

Een – eyes

Frae – from

Fir – for

Guddle – messy and difficult task

Hame - home

Hasnae – hasn't

Heid – head

Herrin heid – Herring head

Hoose – house

Gai - go

Gairden – garden

Gaun – Going

Gey - great as in an amount

Greeting – crying

Guid - good

Howking – digging

Ken – know

Kent - knew

Kilt – killed

Lassie - girl

Lugs – ears

Maw - mother

Mawk – possibly maggot

Mither - mother

Mooth - mouth

Nane – none

Oor - our

Oot – out

Plooks – spots

Naebody - nobody

Nae doot – no doubt

Nae sick – no such

Noo – now

Richt - right

Skint – having no money

Tae - to

Tatties - potatoes

Toon – town

Twa - two

Plooks – spots

Wan – one

Watter - water

Weans – little ones

Wee - little

Whit – what

Wid – would

Wrang - wrong

Wuman – woman

Wunner - wonder

Yer – your

Yeself - yourself

Yin – one

9 781835 382684